Scotland Travel Guide

*Navigate the Best Routes, Cuisine, and Culture
with Confidence. Your Essential Companion to
Unforgettable Experiences and Historic
Landscapes. (Pocket Edition)*

John Patterson

This document is geared towards providing exact and reliable information with regards to the topic and issue covered. The publication is sold with the idea that the publisher is not required to render accounting, officially permitted, or otherwise, qualified services. If advice is necessary, legal or professional, a practiced individual in the profession should be ordered.

From a Declaration of Principles which was accepted and approved equally by a Committee of the American Bar Association and a Committee of Publishers and Associations.

The information provided herein is stated to be truthful and consistent, in that any liability, in terms of inattention or otherwise, by any usage or abuse of any policies, processes, or directions contained within is the solitary and utter responsibility of the recipient reader. Under no circumstances will any legal responsibility or blame be held against the

TABLE OF CONTENT

INTRODUCTION

Welcome to Scotland

Scotland, a land where history whispers through ancient stones and the landscape dances with untamed beauty, beckons travelers with its rich tapestry of traditions, vibrant cities, and breathtaking vistas. From the rolling hills of the Lowlands to the rugged peaks of the Highlands, Scotland offers a journey through time and nature, wrapped in the warmth of its people and the allure of its culture.

As you step onto Scottish soil, the air itself seems infused with the echoes of the past and the promise of adventure. This is a place where every turn unveils a new story, where castles stand sentinel over misty glens, and where the music of bagpipes stirs the soul. The cities, with their blend of ancient and modern, invite exploration. Edinburgh, the capital, is a city of contrasts, where the medieval Old Town and the elegant Georgian New Town coexist in harmony. Climb Arthur's Seat for a panoramic view, or delve into the narrow closes of the Royal Mile to discover hidden gems. Here, history is not confined to museums; it is woven into the very fabric of the city, from the imposing Edinburgh Castle to the Palace of Holyroodhouse.

Venturing west, Glasgow offers a different kind of charm. A city that pulses with creativity and energy, Glasgow is known for its thriving arts scene, vibrant nightlife, and warm, welcoming locals. The architecture here tells a story of its own, from the Victorian grandeur of the city center to the innovative designs of Charles Rennie Mackintosh. Museums and galleries abound, offering glimpses into art, history, and science. Yet, Glasgow is not just a city of culture; it is a city of the people, where the true spirit of Scotland is found in lively conversations over a pint or a cup of tea.

Beyond the cities, the Scottish countryside unfolds in a symphony of landscapes that captivate the imagination. The Highlands, with their dramatic mountains and serene lochs, offer a sense of solitude and majesty that is unmatched. Here, nature reigns supreme, and outdoor enthusiasts will find a paradise of hiking trails, wildlife watching, and opportunities to connect with the land. The iconic Loch Ness, shrouded in mystery, invites you to ponder the legends that have captured the world's imagination.

Scotland's islands, scattered like jewels across the sea, each have their own unique character. The Isle of Skye, with its rugged beauty and mystical allure, calls to adventurers and dreamers alike. The Orkney and Shetland Islands, rich in Norse heritage, offer a glimpse into a different side of Scottish history and culture. Here, the pace of life is slower, the landscapes more untouched, and the connection to nature deeper.

Yet, it is not just the land that defines Scotland; it is its people and their traditions. The Scots are known for their hospitality, their sense of humor, and their pride in their heritage. Festivals and events throughout the year celebrate everything from music and dance to food and drink. The Edinburgh Festival Fringe, the world's largest arts festival, transforms the city into a vibrant stage every August, while the Highland Games showcase traditional sports and the thrill of competition.

Cuisine in Scotland is a journey in itself, with flavors that reflect the land and its bounty. From the hearty comfort of haggis, neeps, and tatties to the delicate complexity of fresh seafood, Scottish food tells a story of tradition and innovation. Whisky, the "water of life," is a quintessential part of the Scottish experience. Distilleries across the country offer tours and tastings, revealing the art and craft behind each dram.

As you travel through Scotland, you will find that it is a country that defies expectation and invites exploration. Each region has its own identity, yet all are united by a shared history and a passion for preserving their unique culture. Whether you are drawn to the bustling cities, the serene countryside, or the remote islands, you will discover that Scotland is a place of endless discovery and unforgettable experiences.

Welcome to a land where the past and present coexist in harmony, where the beauty of nature inspires awe, and where the warmth of the people makes every visitor feel at home. Scotland is more than a destination; it is a journey of the heart and soul, a place where memories are made and stories are shared. As you begin your exploration, let the spirit of Scotland guide you, and may your travels be filled with wonder and joy.

How to Use This Guide

Navigating the wealth of experiences that Scotland offers can be both exhilarating and overwhelming. This guide is crafted to be your steadfast companion, designed to make your journey through Scotland as seamless and enriching as possible. Understanding how to effectively use this guide is your first step towards an unforgettable adventure.

Begin by familiarizing yourself with the table of contents, which is thoughtfully organized to cover various aspects of Scotland. Each chapter is dedicated to exploring specific elements of Scottish culture, geography, and lifestyle, ensuring you have a comprehensive understanding of what to expect. Whether you are a history enthusiast, a nature lover, or a culinary explorer, this guide caters to all interests with detailed insights tailored to each chapter's focus.

When planning your itinerary, use the guide to discover not just the well-trodden paths, but also the hidden gems that make Scotland unique. Each location comes alive with vivid descriptions, offering a sense of place that will help you decide which areas resonate most with your personal travel goals. Pay attention to the sections detailing local customs and traditions, as these will enrich your interactions with the places and people you encounter.

The guide is structured to provide practical advice alongside cultural insights. For example, while exploring Edinburgh's historic landmarks, you will find tips on the best times to visit to avoid crowds, as well as recommendations for nearby dining spots where you can sample local cuisine. This integration of logistics with experience allows you to maximize your time and immerse yourself fully in the local atmosphere.

Scotland's landscapes are as varied as they are breathtaking. The guide includes detailed routes for scenic drives and hikes, complete with maps and difficulty levels to suit all adventurers. Use these sections to plan your outdoor excursions, ensuring you are well-prepared with the right gear and knowledge of weather conditions. The practical travel tips chapter is an essential read before embarking on any journey, offering advice on everything from public transport to sustainable travel practices.

For food enthusiasts, the culinary journey chapter is a treasure trove of information. Discover traditional Scottish dishes and where to find the best local ingredients. The guide includes recommendations for restaurants and cafés that highlight Scotland's diverse culinary scene, from rustic inns serving hearty fare to modern establishments offering innovative twists on classic dishes. If you're interested in deepening your culinary experience, the sections on whisky tasting and cooking classes provide opportunities to engage with Scotland's gastronomic heritage on a deeper level.

Cultural events and festivals offer a window into the soul of Scotland. This guide includes a calendar of major events, such as the Edinburgh Festival Fringe and the Highland Games, providing insights into their history and significance. Use this information to plan your visit around these vibrant celebrations, ensuring you experience the full spectrum of Scottish culture.

As you venture into Scotland's rich history and legends, the guide serves as both a storyteller and educator. The chapters dedicated to ancient sites and myths provide context and background, enhancing your visits to historical landmarks and museums. For those tracing ancestry, practical advice on accessing records and archives is included, helping you connect with your Scottish roots.

The guide's layout is user-friendly, with each chapter designed to stand alone while contributing to the overall narrative of your Scottish adventure. This allows you to dip into different sections as needed, depending on where you are in your journey. The practical travel tips section is a must-read before arrival, covering essential information such as safety, accommodation options, and emergency contacts.

For those seeking unique experiences, the guide highlights off-the-beaten-path adventures that promise authenticity and rarity. Discover hidden villages, engage in local workshops, or participate in seasonal celebrations that bring you closer to the local way of life. The guide also points out volunteer opportunities, allowing you to give back to the communities you visit and enrich your travel experience.

In your hands, this guide becomes more than just a book; it is a gateway to understanding and exploring Scotland with confidence. It is designed to be adaptable, allowing you to tailor your journey to fit your interests and travel style. Whether you are a solo adventurer, traveling with family, or on a romantic getaway, the guide offers something for everyone, ensuring your Scottish adventure is as personalized as it is memorable. Embrace the richness of Scotland, knowing that with this guide, you are well-equipped to navigate its wonders and create lasting memories.

Planning Your Scottish Adventure

Embarking on a journey to Scotland requires thoughtful planning to ensure a seamless and memorable adventure. The diversity of experiences available across the country's landscapes, cities, and cultural offerings demands a well-structured itinerary that caters to your interests and travel style. Whether you're enchanted by the historic allure of ancient castles, the vibrant life of bustling cities, or the serene beauty of natural landscapes, careful preparation will allow you to experience the best that Scotland has to offer.

Begin by determining the duration of your stay, which will significantly influence your itinerary. A week-long visit can provide a taste of both urban and rural Scotland, while a longer stay of two to three weeks allows for a more in-depth exploration. Consider your arrival point, likely to be one of Scotland's major airports in Edinburgh or Glasgow, which will serve as your gateway to the rest of the country.

Next, align your itinerary with your interests. If history captivates you, focus on regions rich in heritage, such as the castles and battlefields of the Highlands or the ancient sites in Orkney. For those drawn to urban experiences, Edinburgh and Glasgow offer a wealth of museums, galleries, and cultural events. Nature enthusiasts will find the Highlands, Isle of Skye, and Cairngorms National Park teeming with opportunities for hiking, wildlife watching, and photography.

Transportation is a crucial aspect of planning your adventure. Scotland's public transport network, including buses and trains, is reliable and covers most major destinations. However, renting a car can provide the freedom to explore remote areas at your own pace, particularly in the Highlands and islands where public transport is less frequent. Ensure you are familiar with driving on the left side of the road and acquire a GPS or detailed maps to navigate the scenic routes.

Accommodation options in Scotland are diverse, ranging from luxury hotels in city centers to cozy bed-and-breakfasts in rural areas. Consider staying in traditional Scottish lodgings, such as a castle hotel or a countryside inn, to enhance your cultural experience. Booking in advance is recommended, especially during peak tourist months and around major festivals.

Seasonality plays a significant role in planning your trip. Scotland's weather can be unpredictable, but each season offers its own charm. Summer, from June to August, provides long daylight hours and is ideal for outdoor activities, although popular sites may be crowded. Spring and autumn, with their milder temperatures and vibrant landscapes, are perfect for exploring the countryside. Winter, while colder and darker, offers the chance to experience Scotland's festive spirit, with Christmas markets and Hogmanay celebrations.

Pack appropriately for Scotland's variable weather, with layers that can be added or removed as needed. Waterproof clothing and sturdy footwear are essential, especially if you plan on hiking or spending time outdoors. A travel adapter for UK plug sockets and a portable charger for your electronic devices will ensure you stay connected and powered throughout your journey.

Scotland is famed for its festivals, which provide unique insights into local culture. Plan your visit to coincide with events like the Edinburgh Festival Fringe, the Highland Games, or the Royal Edinburgh Military Tattoo, each offering a distinctive experience. These festivals often attract large crowds, so purchasing tickets in advance and arranging accommodation early is advisable.

While planning your adventure, consider incorporating guided tours to enhance your understanding of Scotland's history and natural beauty. Walking tours in cities like Edinburgh and Glasgow can offer a local perspective, revealing hidden stories and lesser-known sites. In the Highlands, guided hikes or wildlife tours provide safety and expert knowledge that enrich your experience.

Food and drink are integral to the Scottish experience, and planning your culinary journey is a delightful part of your adventure. Research local dishes and restaurants to include in your itinerary, ensuring you sample traditional fare like haggis, Cullen skink, and cranachan. Whisky enthusiasts should map out distilleries for tastings and tours, particularly in regions like Speyside and Islay known for their distinctive spirits.

Scotland's rich history offers opportunities for those interested in tracing their ancestry. If this is part of your journey, prepare by gathering family records and identifying key locations or archives to visit. Many areas offer genealogical resources and experts who can assist in uncovering your Scottish roots.

As you finalize your plans, remain flexible and open to spontaneous discoveries. While a well-structured itinerary ensures you cover your must-see destinations, some of the most memorable experiences can arise from unplanned detours or local recommendations. Engage with locals, who are often eager to share their stories and tips, adding a personal dimension to your travels.

Finally, consider the principles of sustainable travel as you explore Scotland. Support local businesses, respect natural habitats, and minimize your environmental impact by reducing waste and conserving resources. By doing so, you contribute to the preservation of Scotland's unique landscapes and cultural heritage for future generations.

With your plans in place, you are ready to embark on a journey through a land of legends and landscapes, where every corner holds a story waiting to be discovered. Scotland awaits with open arms, promising an adventure filled with history, beauty, and unforgettable moments.

CHAPTER 1: THE HEART OF SCOTLAND - EDINBURGH

Exploring Edinburgh's Historic Landmarks

Edinburgh, the capital city of Scotland, is a captivating blend of history, architecture, and culture. Its skyline is dominated by the dramatic presence of Edinburgh Castle, perched atop Castle Rock. This fortress is not just a historic monument but a symbol of resilience and strength. As you wander through its ancient corridors, the Great Hall and the Stone of Destiny reveal tales of Scottish royalty and the nation's turbulent past. The Crown Jewels, on display, dazzle with their beauty and significance, each piece a testament to the country's storied heritage.

The Royal Mile, stretching from the castle to the Palace of Holyroodhouse, is a journey through time. This vibrant thoroughfare is lined with medieval buildings, each with its own story etched into the stone. St Giles' Cathedral, with its stunning crown spire, stands as a beacon of faith and history. Inside, the Thistle Chapel captures attention with its intricate carvings and beautiful stained glass, offering a moment of serenity amid the bustling street outside.

As you continue down the Royal Mile, the historic closes and wynds—narrow alleyways that branch off the main street—invite exploration. These hidden gems, such as Mary King's Close, offer a glimpse into the lives of Edinburgh's past residents. Guided tours reveal the stories of those who lived and worked in these now underground streets, providing a haunting yet fascinating perspective on the city's social history.

The Palace of Holyroodhouse, at the opposite end of the Royal Mile, serves as the official residence of the British monarch in Scotland. Its baroque architecture and lush gardens provide a stark contrast to the rugged castle at the other end of the Mile. As you explore its opulent rooms, the history of Mary, Queen of Scots, is brought to life. The palace's connections to both royal drama and everyday life make it an essential stop for history enthusiasts.

Adjacent to the palace, the Scottish Parliament building presents a modern architectural marvel. Designed by Enric Miralles, its unique structure contrasts with Edinburgh's traditional skyline. Visitors can take guided tours to learn about Scotland's political landscape and the building's sustainable design features, which reflect the country's commitment to innovation.

Arthur's Seat, an extinct volcano and the highest point in Holyrood Park, offers panoramic views of the city and beyond. The hike to the summit is a rewarding experience, providing a natural escape from the urban environment. The landscape around Arthur's Seat is dotted with historical sites, including the ruins of St Anthony's Chapel, adding layers of intrigue to the scenic beauty.

Calton Hill, another vantage point, is home to several iconic monuments. The National Monument, inspired by the Parthenon, stands as a symbol of Scotland's cultural aspirations. The Nelson Monument and the Dugald Stewart Monument offer additional insight into the city's historical narratives. As you stand on the hill, the view encompasses the Old Town and the New Town, illustrating the city's evolution over the centuries.

The New Town, a masterpiece of Georgian architecture, represents Edinburgh's Enlightenment-era grandeur. Its elegant streets, such as George Street and Princes Street, are lined with symmetrical terraces and stately buildings. The Scottish National Gallery, located here, houses an impressive collection of art, from Renaissance masterpieces to modern works by Scottish artists. It provides a cultural counterpoint to the historic landmarks, showcasing the breadth of Scotland's artistic heritage.

A visit to the Grassmarket area, nestled beneath the castle, reveals a lively neighborhood steeped in history. This former medieval marketplace is now a hub of activity, with pubs, shops, and cafes lining its cobbled streets. The area's rich history, including its role as a site for public executions, contrasts with its current vibrant atmosphere, making it a fascinating area to explore.

For those interested in literary history, the Writers' Museum provides insights into the lives and works of Scotland's literary giants: Robert Burns, Sir Walter Scott, and Robert Louis Stevenson. Housed in a 17th-century building, the museum's exhibits offer a personal connection to the authors who shaped Scottish literature.

Edinburgh is renowned for its ghostly tales and supernatural legends. The city's darker past comes to life on evening ghost tours, which explore haunted sites and chilling stories. These tours offer an alternative perspective on the city's history, blending folklore with historical fact.

As you delve into Edinburgh's historic landmarks, the city's layers of history unfold in a tapestry of stories and experiences. Each site, from the imposing castle to the serene palace gardens, contributes to the narrative of a city that has played a pivotal role in Scotland's history. The blend of old and new, tradition and innovation, creates a unique atmosphere that captivates visitors and leaves a lasting impression.

In exploring these landmarks, you not only witness Scotland's past but also engage with the living history that continues to shape its present and future. Edinburgh's charm lies in its ability to transport you through time while inviting you to become part of its ongoing story. Whether it's the echoes of bagpipes on the Royal Mile or the panoramic vistas from its hills, the city offers a rich tapestry of experiences waiting to be discovered.

Discovering Local Cuisine and Dining Spots

Edinburgh's culinary scene is a vibrant tapestry of traditional Scottish flavors interwoven with global influences, offering a delightful journey for the taste buds. The city is a hub of gastronomic innovation, where chefs celebrate Scotland's rich larder of fresh, local ingredients. From haggis to haute cuisine,

Edinburgh's dining spots cater to all tastes and preferences, ensuring a memorable culinary adventure.

Begin your exploration with a taste of traditional Scottish fare. Haggis, perhaps the most iconic dish, is a must-try for any visitor. This savory pudding made of sheep's offal mixed with oatmeal, onions, and spices, is often accompanied by neeps (turnips) and tatties (potatoes). While some may approach it with trepidation, many find haggis to be a surprisingly delicious experience. For an authentic taste, consider visiting a local pub or restaurant that specializes in regional cuisine, such as The Royal McGregor on the Royal Mile, where haggis is served with whisky sauce for an added touch of indulgence.

Seafood lovers will find Edinburgh a paradise, with its proximity to the North Sea ensuring a bounty of fresh catches. Smoked salmon, langoustines, and scallops are just a few of the delicacies that grace the menus of the city's eateries. Head to The Ship on the Shore in Leith, known for its exceptional seafood platters and maritime ambiance. This charming harborside restaurant captures the essence of Scotland's coastal heritage, offering dishes that highlight the natural flavors of the sea with minimal adornment.

For those seeking modern Scottish cuisine, a visit to The Kitchin is essential. Chef Tom Kitchin's Michelin-starred restaurant in Leith epitomizes the farm-to-table philosophy, with dishes that celebrate seasonal ingredients sourced from local suppliers. The menu is a testament to Scotland's culinary evolution, blending traditional techniques with contemporary flair. Each dish is a masterpiece, reflecting the rich diversity of Scotland's natural produce, from Highland venison to foraged herbs.

Edinburgh's international dining scene is equally impressive, with a variety of options reflecting the city's cosmopolitan nature. For a taste of Italy, Contini George Street offers a menu brimming with authentic Italian flavors, made with ingredients imported directly from Italy. The elegant setting complements the vibrant dishes, making it a perfect spot for a leisurely meal. Similarly, Chaophraya, with its panoramic views of the city skyline, serves up Thai cuisine infused with bold flavors and aromatic spices, providing a sensory journey far beyond Scotland's borders.

Vegetarians and vegans will find plenty of options in Edinburgh, as the city has embraced plant-based dining with enthusiasm. Hendersons, a pioneer in vegetarian cuisine since the 1960s, offers a delightful array of dishes in a casual, welcoming environment. Their menu focuses on fresh, organic produce, crafted into creative and satisfying meals. For a more contemporary take on vegan dining, David Bann's restaurant provides an imaginative menu that showcases the versatility of vegetables, with globally inspired dishes that surprise and delight.

No culinary journey in Edinburgh is complete without indulging in its sweet offerings. Scottish shortbread, with its buttery richness, is a classic treat that can be found in many cafes and bakeries. For a more indulgent experience, visit Mimi's Bakehouse, where an array of cakes, scones, and pastries await. Their afternoon tea, complete with delicate sandwiches and freshly baked goods, offers a quintessentially British experience in a cozy setting.

For those interested in exploring Edinburgh's vibrant food markets, Stockbridge Market is a must-visit. Held every Sunday, this bustling market features a variety of stalls offering artisanal goods, fresh produce, and street food from around the world. Here, you can sample cheeses, chutneys, and baked goods, all while soaking in the lively atmosphere of one of Edinburgh's most charming neighborhoods.

Whisky, Scotland's national drink, is an integral part of the dining experience. Many restaurants and pubs offer extensive whisky lists, allowing you to savor the diverse flavors of this beloved spirit. For a more immersive experience, consider a visit to The Scotch Whisky Experience, where you can learn about the whisky-making process and enjoy guided tastings. Alternatively, visit one of Edinburgh's whisky bars, such as The Bow Bar or Whiski Rooms, where knowledgeable staff can guide you through the nuances of different malts and blends.

As you dine your way through Edinburgh, take the opportunity to engage with the city's culinary community. Many restaurants offer cooking classes or tasting events, providing an insider's view into the art of Scottish cooking. These experiences not only enhance your understanding of local cuisine but also offer a chance to connect with the passionate individuals who are shaping Edinburgh's food scene.

Edinburgh's dining landscape is as diverse as its historic streets, offering a culinary journey that is both satisfying and enlightening. With each meal, you partake in a tradition of hospitality and innovation, savoring the flavors that define Scotland's rich and varied culinary heritage. Whether you are enjoying a hearty plate of haggis in a cozy pub, sampling seafood by the harbor, or savoring a Michelin-starred experience, the city's vibrant food culture promises to leave you with lasting memories and a deeper appreciation for the flavors of Scotland.

The Best Walking Tours and Trails

Edinburgh, with its rich history and stunning landscapes, is a city best explored on foot. Walking tours and trails offer an intimate glimpse into the character of this vibrant city, allowing you to tread the same paths as historical figures, explore hidden alleys, and immerse yourself in breathtaking views. Whether you are a history buff, a nature enthusiast, or simply a curious traveler, Edinburgh has a walking tour or trail to suit your interests.

Begin your journey with a classic: the Old Town Walking Tour. This tour meanders through the heart of Edinburgh's historic district, where cobblestone streets echo with stories of the past. As you navigate the Royal Mile, your guide will unravel tales of monarchs, writers, and everyday Edinburgh folk. Stops include the hauntingly beautiful St Giles' Cathedral, the intriguing closes and wynds, and the infamous Grassmarket, once a site for public executions. The tour often concludes at the majestic Edinburgh Castle, offering panoramic views of the city below.

For those intrigued by the city's darker side, the Ghosts and Ghouls Walking Tour provides a thrilling experience. Edinburgh's reputation as one of Europe's most haunted cities comes to life as you venture into its shadowy corners. Explore the eerie underground vaults and hear chilling stories of restless spirits and mysterious happenings. Guides, often in period costume, deliver these tales with a theatrical flair that adds to the spine-tingling atmosphere.

Nature lovers should not miss a hike up Arthur's Seat, an ancient volcano that provides a natural escape within the city. The ascent begins in Holyrood Park, where trails wind through rugged terrain to the summit. As you climb, the city gradually unfolds beneath you, offering spectacular views that reward your efforts. The landscape is dotted with historical sites, such as the ruins of St Anthony's Chapel, which add layers of interest to the hike. Whether you're seeking a peaceful retreat or an invigorating challenge, Arthur's Seat delivers both.

Calton Hill is another favorite for walkers, known for its iconic monuments and sweeping vistas. The short but steep climb is rewarded with a panoramic view of Edinburgh's skyline, including landmarks like the Nelson Monument and the National Monument. The hill is a popular spot for photographers, especially at sunrise or sunset when the city is bathed in golden light. The walk is easily accessible from the city center, making it a perfect choice for those with limited time.

For a more leisurely stroll, the Water of Leith Walkway offers a tranquil escape from the urban hustle. This picturesque trail follows the river as it winds through the city, passing through leafy suburbs and quaint villages. Along the way, you'll encounter landmarks such as the Scottish National Gallery of Modern Art and the charming Dean Village, with its idyllic setting and historic architecture. The walkway provides a refreshing contrast to the bustling streets, allowing you to experience a different side of Edinburgh.

Those interested in literary history will find the Edinburgh Literary Pub Tour both educational and entertaining. This unique tour combines storytelling with visits to historic pubs, where writers like Robert Burns and Sir Walter Scott found inspiration. Led by actors portraying literary characters, the tour offers insights into Scotland's rich literary heritage while providing ample opportunity to sample local ales and whiskies. The lively atmosphere and engaging narratives make it a favorite among literature lovers.

For a journey into Edinburgh's past, the Real Mary King's Close tour offers a fascinating glimpse into the city's hidden history. Descend into the underground streets of the 17th century, where everyday life unfolded beneath the bustling city above. The guided tour reveals the stories of the residents who lived in these narrow closes, providing a unique perspective on Edinburgh's social history. The experience is both immersive and enlightening, shedding light on the challenges and triumphs of the city's past inhabitants.

If you're keen to explore the city's diverse neighborhoods, consider the Leith Walk and Shore tour. This vibrant area, once an independent port town, is now a thriving part of Edinburgh with a distinct character. The tour takes you through Leith's lively streets, showcasing its eclectic mix of shops, cafes, and cultural sites. Highlights include the historic Leith Docks and the Shore, known for its waterfront restaurants and colorful murals. The tour captures the essence of Leith's transformation from a gritty port to a cultural hotspot.

No exploration of Edinburgh would be complete without a visit to the New Town, a masterpiece of Georgian architecture. The New Town Walking Tour guides you through elegant streets such as George Street and Princes Street, lined with grand terraces and historic buildings. The tour includes stops at notable sites like the Scott Monument and the Royal Scottish Academy, offering insights into the city's Enlightenment-era development. The New Town's sophisticated charm and architectural beauty make it a must-see for any visitor.

Edinburgh's walking tours and trails offer a diverse range of experiences that cater to all interests and fitness levels. Whether you're delving into the city's haunted history, enjoying its natural beauty, or exploring its cultural landmarks, walking provides a unique and immersive way to connect with Edinburgh's many facets. As you traverse the city's streets and paths, you'll discover the stories and sights that make Edinburgh a truly enchanting destination.

Festivals and Cultural Events

Edinburgh is renowned worldwide as a city of festivals, a place where culture, creativity, and celebration converge in a dazzling array of events throughout the year. From the world's largest arts festival to intimate local gatherings, these events offer a vibrant tapestry of experiences that reflect the city's dynamic spirit and rich heritage. For both locals and visitors, Edinburgh's festivals and cultural events provide a unique opportunity to immerse oneself in the city's artistic and social fabric.

The Edinburgh Festival Fringe, held every August, is the crown jewel of the city's festival calendar. Known as the largest arts festival in the world, the Fringe transforms the city into a bustling hub of creativity. Performers from across the globe descend on Edinburgh, presenting thousands of shows in venues ranging from grand theaters to intimate cafes and even the streets themselves. The atmosphere is electric, with a diverse program that includes theater, comedy, music, dance, and cabaret. For those seeking the unexpected, the Fringe offers a platform for experimentation and innovation, where emerging artists share the stage with established names.

Running concurrently with the Fringe is the Edinburgh International Festival, which showcases a curated selection of the finest in classical music, opera, dance, and theater. Founded in 1947 with the aim of providing a platform for cultural exchange and reconciliation, the festival continues to attract world-class performers and audiences. The grandeur of venues like the Usher Hall and the Festival Theatre adds to the sense of occasion, offering a more formal counterpoint to the Fringe's eclectic energy.

Another highlight of the festival season is the Royal Edinburgh Military Tattoo, a spectacular display of military pageantry set against the backdrop of Edinburgh Castle. This event is a feast for the senses, combining precision marching, music, and fireworks in a breathtaking display of skill and tradition. Each year, the Tattoo features performers from around the world, celebrating military and cultural heritage with a uniquely Scottish flair.

The Edinburgh International Book Festival, held in Charlotte Square Gardens, is a haven for literary enthusiasts. This event brings together authors, thinkers, and readers for a series of discussions, readings, and debates. With a program that spans fiction, non-fiction, and poetry, the festival fosters a spirit of intellectual curiosity and dialogue. The relaxed garden setting provides an ideal environment for exploring new ideas and engaging with the literary community.

In December, Edinburgh embraces the festive spirit with its Christmas and Hogmanay celebrations. The city's Christmas markets, ice rinks, and light displays create a magical atmosphere, drawing visitors and locals alike. Hogmanay, the Scottish New Year celebration, is legendary for its exuberance and scale. The festivities include torchlight processions, concerts, and a spectacular fireworks display over the castle, culminating in a street party that welcomes the new year with music, dancing, and camaraderie.

Beyond these major events, Edinburgh hosts a variety of smaller festivals that cater to diverse interests. The Edinburgh Jazz and Blues Festival, held in July, attracts top musicians from around the world, offering performances that span genres from traditional jazz to contemporary fusion. The vibrant atmosphere spills into the streets, with free open-air concerts and late-night jam sessions.

For film lovers, the Edinburgh International Film Festival, established in 1947, is a must-visit. Renowned for its focus on innovation and discovery, the festival showcases a diverse range of films, including premieres, retrospectives, and experimental works. The event provides a platform for filmmakers to connect with audiences, fostering a sense of community and shared appreciation for the art of cinema.

The city's cultural calendar also includes the Edinburgh Art Festival, a visual arts celebration that takes place in August. This festival features exhibitions, commissions, and events across the city, highlighting both established and emerging artists. With a focus on contemporary art, the festival encourages exploration and dialogue, inviting audiences to engage with new perspectives and ideas.

For those interested in science and technology, the Edinburgh Science Festival, held in April, offers a fascinating exploration of the wonders of the natural world. With a program that includes interactive exhibits, workshops, and talks, the festival caters to all ages and interests. It provides a platform for scientists and innovators to share their work, inspiring curiosity and discovery.

The cultural events in Edinburgh extend beyond the confines of traditional festivals, with a year-round schedule of concerts, theater productions, and exhibitions. Venues like the Scottish National Gallery, the Queen's Hall, and the Royal Lyceum Theatre host performances and exhibitions that enrich the city's cultural landscape. These events offer an opportunity to experience Edinburgh's artistic vibrancy on a more intimate scale.

Engaging with Edinburgh's festivals and cultural events offers more than just entertainment; it provides a window into the city's soul. These gatherings celebrate the creativity, diversity, and resilience that define Edinburgh, fostering connections between people and ideas. Whether you're attending a world-class performance, exploring a thought-provoking exhibition, or simply enjoying the festive atmosphere, the city's cultural offerings promise to leave a lasting impression.

In planning your visit to Edinburgh, timing your trip to coincide with one of these festivals can enhance your experience, offering a unique perspective on the city's character and charm. Each event, with its distinct flavor and focus, contributes to the rich tapestry of Edinburgh's cultural identity, ensuring that there is always something new to discover and enjoy.

Shopping and Souvenirs

Edinburgh is a city that offers a unique shopping experience, blending traditional Scottish heritage with contemporary style. From quaint boutiques to bustling markets, the capital of Scotland presents a diverse array of shopping opportunities for every taste and budget. Whether you are seeking high-end fashion, artisanal crafts, or quintessential Scottish keepsakes, Edinburgh's shopping districts are the perfect places to explore.

Start your shopping adventure on Princes Street, the city's main shopping thoroughfare. Here, you will find an array of well-known high-street brands and department stores, offering everything from fashion to electronics. The iconic Jenners department store, a fixture since 1838, is a must-visit for its elegant architecture and wide selection of luxury goods. As you stroll along this bustling street, take in the stunning views of Edinburgh Castle and the historic Old Town, providing a picturesque backdrop to your shopping excursion.

For a more eclectic shopping experience, head to the Grassmarket area. Nestled beneath the imposing Edinburgh Castle, this historic part of the city is known for its independent shops and vibrant atmosphere. The Grassmarket is home to a variety of vintage stores, artisan studios, and quirky boutiques, offering a treasure trove of unique finds. From handcrafted jewelry and bespoke clothing to rare books and antiques, the Grassmarket is a haven for those in search of one-of-a-kind items.

Venturing into the New Town, George Street presents a sophisticated shopping scene with a mix of designer boutiques and stylish cafes. This elegant street is lined with Georgian architecture, housing a range of high-end retailers and chic brands. For lovers of luxury, George Street offers an exquisite selection of fashion, accessories, and cosmetics, ensuring a refined shopping experience.

For those interested in supporting local artisans, the Stockbridge Market is a delightful destination. Held every Sunday, this bustling market features a variety of stalls offering handmade goods, fresh produce, and gourmet treats.

Here, you can find unique souvenirs such as artisanal cheeses, handcrafted candles, and beautifully crafted ceramics. The market's lively atmosphere and friendly vendors make it a pleasant place to spend a leisurely afternoon.

No visit to Edinburgh would be complete without a foray into the world of Scottish textiles. The city is renowned for its high-quality tweeds and tartans, with numerous shops offering these traditional fabrics in contemporary designs. Johnston of Elgin, located on Multrees Walk, is a prestigious brand known for its luxurious cashmere and wool products. Whether you are looking for a classic tartan scarf or a stylish tweed jacket, you will find an array of options that blend heritage with modern fashion.

For a truly Scottish shopping experience, venture to the Royal Mile, where you will find a plethora of souvenir shops offering everything from kilts to whisky. While some stores cater to tourists with mass-produced items, there are also hidden gems that offer authentic Scottish crafts. Look for shops that specialize in local products, such as Harris Tweed, hand-knit woolens, and traditional Celtic jewelry. These items not only make wonderful gifts but also serve as lasting mementos of your time in Scotland.

Whisky enthusiasts will find Edinburgh a paradise for tasting and purchasing Scotland's national drink. Specialist whisky shops, such as Royal Mile Whiskies and Cadenhead's, offer an extensive selection of single malts and blends, along with expert advice from knowledgeable staff. Many stores provide tasting sessions, allowing you to sample a range of whiskies before making your purchase. A bottle of fine Scotch whisky makes a perfect souvenir or gift, embodying the spirit and tradition of Scotland.

For book lovers, Edinburgh's literary heritage is reflected in its numerous independent bookshops. Armchair Books, located in the West Port area, is a charming second-hand bookstore filled with treasures waiting to be discovered. Nearby, the Edinburgh Bookshop offers a carefully curated selection of new titles, with an emphasis on Scottish authors and local interest. These bookstores provide a cozy retreat for browsing and discovering new literary gems.

As you explore Edinburgh's shopping scene, take the time to appreciate the city's commitment to sustainability and ethical practices. Many shops and markets focus on locally sourced, eco-friendly products, reflecting a growing awareness of environmental issues. By choosing sustainable and ethically produced items, you can support Edinburgh's vibrant community of artisans and entrepreneurs while making a positive impact on the environment.

Edinburgh's shopping districts offer a diverse range of experiences that cater to all tastes and preferences. Whether you are seeking high fashion, artisanal crafts, or traditional Scottish souvenirs, the city's shops and markets provide a wealth of options to explore. As you wander through Edinburgh's streets, you will discover a rich tapestry of culture and creativity, reflected in the unique and varied offerings of its many retailers.

CHAPTER 2: VIBRANT GLASGOW

Glasgow's Art and Music Scene

Glasgow, a city pulsating with creativity and energy, stands as a beacon of the arts in Scotland. Its vibrant art and music scene is a testament to its rich cultural heritage and dynamic present. Whether you're drawn to the avant-garde or the classical, Glasgow offers a myriad of experiences that showcase its commitment to artistic expression and musical innovation.

The city's art scene is diverse and influential, with institutions that cater to a wide range of tastes. The Kelvingrove Art Gallery and Museum is a cornerstone of Glasgow's cultural landscape. Housing an extensive collection of art and historical artifacts, it offers a journey through both local and international art history. The museum's eclectic displays range from the dramatic paintings of the Glasgow Boys to the surreal works of Salvador Dalí, including the renowned "Christ of St John of the Cross." This gallery is not merely a repository of art but a vibrant space where history and creativity converge.

For those intrigued by contemporary art, the Gallery of Modern Art (GoMA) is a must-visit. Located in the heart of the city, GoMA presents cutting-edge exhibitions that challenge and inspire. The gallery is known for its dynamic programming, which often includes interactive installations and thought-provoking pieces that engage with current social and political themes. GoMA's commitment to showcasing a diverse range of artists makes it a pivotal space for contemporary art dialogue in the UK.

The city's art scene extends beyond its galleries. The vibrant street art that adorns Glasgow's walls and buildings speaks to its spirit of rebellion and innovation. The Glasgow Mural Trail is a testament to this, offering a self-guided tour through the city's streets to discover stunning murals that celebrate local culture and history. These artworks transform the urban landscape into an open-air gallery, reflecting the city's unique identity and sense of community.

Glasgow's music scene is equally dynamic, with a reputation for nurturing talent and innovation. The city has produced renowned bands such as Belle and Sebastian, Franz Ferdinand, and Mogwai, each contributing to Glasgow's status as a music powerhouse. Live music venues abound, offering everything from intimate gigs to grand performances.

King Tut's Wah Wah Hut is legendary in the music world. This iconic venue has been the launching pad for many successful careers, including Oasis, who were famously signed here. The intimate setting provides an up-close experience with emerging artists, making it a favorite among music enthusiasts. The venue's storied history and vibrant atmosphere encapsulate the energy and passion that define Glasgow's music scene.

The Barrowland Ballroom, affectionately known as "The Barras," is another iconic venue that has hosted countless legendary performances. Known for its distinctive sprung dance floor and electric atmosphere, The Barras is a rite of passage for both bands and fans. Its eclectic lineup includes rock, indie, and everything in between, reflecting the city's diverse musical tastes.

For those seeking a more classical music experience, the Royal Concert Hall provides a venue for world-class performances. Home to the Royal Scottish National Orchestra, the hall's acoustics and grandeur make it a premier location for orchestral concerts and musical events. Its varied program includes classical masterpieces, contemporary compositions, and global music, offering something for every listener.

Glasgow's music festivals are another highlight of its cultural calendar. Celtic Connections, held every January, is a celebration of Celtic music and its global connections. The festival features an impressive lineup of artists from around the world, showcasing the versatility and enduring appeal of Celtic sounds. With concerts, workshops, and late-night sessions, Celtic Connections offers a deeply immersive experience in the heart of winter.

The TRNSMT Festival, held on Glasgow Green, is a newer addition to the city's festival scene but has quickly become a staple for music lovers. Featuring a lineup of top international and local acts, TRNSMT captures the vibrancy and diversity of contemporary music. The festival's open-air setting and lively crowds create an unforgettable atmosphere, underscoring Glasgow's status as a music capital.

Beyond formal venues and festivals, Glasgow's music scene thrives in its pubs and clubs. The city's nightlife is legendary, with venues like Nice N Sleazy and The Hug and Pint offering eclectic lineups and a welcoming atmosphere. These spaces foster a sense of community, where locals and visitors can connect over a shared love of music.

Glasgow's commitment to the arts is also evident in its educational institutions. The Glasgow School of Art, one of the leading art schools in the UK, has produced generations of influential artists and designers. Its striking Mackintosh building, designed by Charles Rennie Mackintosh, is a masterpiece of modern architecture and a symbol of the city's dedication to artistic excellence.

The city's universities offer robust music programs, nurturing the next generation of musicians and composers. These institutions provide a fertile ground for creativity, where students can experiment and collaborate, contributing to Glasgow's vibrant cultural scene.

Engaging with Glasgow's art and music scene offers more than just entertainment; it provides a window into the city's soul. The creativity and passion that permeate Glasgow's galleries, venues, and streets are a testament to its resilient spirit and cultural depth. Whether you're exploring groundbreaking art exhibitions, experiencing live music in an iconic venue, or simply soaking in the city's vibrant atmosphere, Glasgow promises an enriching journey through its artistic and musical landscape.

Must-Visit Museums and Galleries

Glasgow, a city rich in history and culture, boasts an impressive array of museums and galleries that reflect its vibrant heritage and contemporary spirit. These institutions offer a window into the city's past and present, showcasing everything from ancient artifacts to cutting-edge art. For anyone visiting Glasgow, these must-visit museums and galleries provide a fascinating journey through time and creativity, each with its own unique story to tell.

Kelvingrove Art Gallery and Museum is perhaps the most iconic of Glasgow's cultural institutions. Nestled in the picturesque West End, this grand building houses an eclectic collection of over 8,000 objects. From the moment you step inside, you're greeted by a diverse array of exhibits, ranging from natural history and world cultures to fine art and Scottish history. Highlights include the stunning Salvador Dalí masterpiece, "Christ of St John of the Cross," and the awe-inspiring arms and armor collection. The museum's interactive displays and family-friendly activities make it a perfect destination for visitors of all ages, ensuring a memorable and engaging experience.

The Riverside Museum, designed by the renowned architect Zaha Hadid, offers a modern and dynamic exploration of transport and travel. Situated on the banks of the River Clyde, this museum presents an impressive collection of vehicles, from vintage cars and bicycles to locomotives and ships. Each exhibit invites you to explore the stories behind Glasgow's rich maritime and industrial heritage. The museum's interactive displays engage visitors in the mechanics and history of transportation, providing a hands-on experience that captivates both young and old. The adjacent Tall Ship, the Glenlee, further enriches the visit, offering a glimpse into life aboard a historic sailing vessel.

The Hunterian Museum and Art Gallery, located on the University of Glasgow's campus, is Scotland's oldest public museum. Founded in 1807, it is home to an extraordinary collection of scientific instruments, geological specimens, and Roman artifacts. The Hunterian Art Gallery boasts an impressive array of works by renowned artists, including James McNeill Whistler and Charles Rennie Mackintosh. The Mackintosh House, a meticulous recreation of the artist's former home, offers a unique insight into his life and work, showcasing his signature style and design. This museum and gallery provide a rich and varied experience, combining art, science, and history in a single visit.

For contemporary art enthusiasts, the Gallery of Modern Art (GoMA) is a must-see. Situated in the heart of the city, GoMA occupies a neoclassical building that once served as the home of a wealthy tobacco lord. Today, it hosts a dynamic program of exhibitions and events, featuring both local and international artists. The gallery's focus on contemporary issues and innovative art forms makes it a thought-provoking destination for those interested in the cutting edge of artistic expression. Its central location also makes it a convenient stop for those exploring the city's vibrant cultural scene.

Scotland Street School Museum, designed by Charles Rennie Mackintosh, offers a fascinating glimpse into the history of education in Glasgow. This beautifully preserved building, once a functioning school, now serves as a museum dedicated to showcasing the evolution of Scottish education. Visitors can explore reconstructed classrooms from different eras, complete with authentic furnishings and educational materials. The museum's interactive exhibits provide a hands-on experience, allowing visitors to step back in time and experience school life as it was in the past. Mackintosh's architectural genius is evident throughout the building, making it a must-visit for fans of his work.

The People's Palace and Winter Gardens, located in Glasgow Green, celebrate the social history of Glasgow and its people. This museum offers a captivating journey through the city's past, highlighting the lives and stories of ordinary Glaswegians. Exhibits cover a range of topics, from the city's industrial heritage to its vibrant cultural traditions. The adjacent Winter Gardens, housed in a beautiful Victorian glasshouse, provide a tranquil oasis filled with exotic plants and flowers. Together, the People's Palace and Winter Gardens offer a unique perspective on the city's history, emphasizing the resilience and creativity of its inhabitants.

Glasgow's museums and galleries are not limited to the traditional; the city's thriving arts scene also includes a range of smaller, independent spaces that offer unique and often experimental exhibitions. The Tramway, located in the Southside, is one such venue. Originally a tram depot, this contemporary arts space now hosts a diverse program of exhibitions, performances, and events. Its focus on interdisciplinary and innovative art makes it a hub for creative exploration and artistic collaboration.

Street Level Photoworks, situated in the city center, is another gem for art enthusiasts. This gallery specializes in contemporary photography, showcasing the work of both emerging and established photographers. Its exhibitions often explore social and political themes, offering a platform for critical engagement and dialogue. The gallery also provides workshops and resources for photographers, supporting the development of new talent and fostering a vibrant photographic community.

For those interested in architecture and design, the Lighthouse is an essential stop. This center for design and architecture celebrates Scotland's creative industries, offering exhibitions, events, and workshops that explore the relationship between design and everyday life. The building itself, designed by Charles Rennie Mackintosh, is a masterpiece of innovative architecture, featuring a distinctive spiral staircase that leads to a panoramic viewing platform. From here, visitors can enjoy stunning views of the city skyline, providing a fitting conclusion to a day of cultural exploration.

Glasgow's museums and galleries offer a rich tapestry of experiences, each contributing to the city's reputation as a cultural capital. Whether you're interested in art, history, science, or design, these institutions provide a diverse and engaging exploration of Glasgow's heritage and innovation. As you wander through these spaces, you'll discover the stories and creativity that define this vibrant city, ensuring a memorable and enriching visit.

Culinary Delights in Glasgow

Glasgow's culinary scene is as vibrant and diverse as the city itself, offering a tantalizing array of flavors that reflect its multicultural heritage. From traditional Scottish fare to innovative global cuisine, Glasgow's food landscape is a feast for the senses, inviting exploration and discovery at every turn. Whether you're a seasoned foodie or a curious traveler, the city's culinary delights promise an unforgettable gastronomic journey.

Begin your exploration with a taste of traditional Scottish cuisine, which is deeply rooted in the country's history and landscape. Haggis, Scotland's national dish, is a must-try for those seeking an authentic Scottish experience. This savory pudding, made from sheep's offal mixed with oatmeal, suet, and spices, is traditionally served with neeps (turnips) and tatties (potatoes). Many restaurants in Glasgow offer their own take on this classic dish, with some even offering vegetarian versions that capture the essence of the original.

For seafood lovers, Glasgow's proximity to the coast ensures a plentiful supply of fresh, high-quality seafood. The city's fishmongers and restaurants showcase a diverse selection, from succulent smoked salmon to plump scallops and tender langoustines. A visit to The Finnieston, located in the trendy Finnieston neighborhood, provides an opportunity to savor expertly prepared seafood dishes in a chic, contemporary setting. With a focus on sustainability and seasonality, The

Finnieston offers a menu that celebrates the bounty of Scotland's waters.

A visit to Glasgow would not be complete without indulging in a hearty Scottish breakfast. This traditional meal typically includes bacon, eggs, sausage, black pudding, and tattie scones, often accompanied by baked beans and toast. Many local cafes and pubs offer their own versions of this satisfying breakfast, providing a perfect start to a day of exploration. The Wilson Street Pantry, located in the Merchant City, is renowned for its delicious and generously portioned Scottish breakfast, served in a cozy and welcoming atmosphere.

Beyond traditional fare, Glasgow's culinary scene is a melting pot of global influences, reflecting the city's diverse population and cosmopolitan spirit. The vibrant West End is home to a plethora of international eateries, offering flavors from around the world. For an authentic taste of Italy, head to Eusebi Deli, where you'll find a delectable selection of homemade pasta, artisan cheeses, and freshly baked pastries. This family-run establishment combines a deli and a restaurant, creating a convivial space where diners can enjoy a taste of la dolce vita.

For those craving the bold and aromatic flavors of India, Mother India's Café is a must-visit. This popular eatery offers a tapas-style menu, allowing diners to sample a variety of dishes, from spicy curries to fragrant biryanis. The relaxed and informal setting makes it an ideal spot for sharing a meal with friends, while the inventive menu showcases the best of Indian cuisine with a contemporary twist.

Glasgow is also home to a burgeoning street food scene, with markets and pop-up events offering a diverse array of culinary delights. The Big Feed, held monthly in a converted warehouse in Govan, is one of the city's largest indoor street food markets. Here, you can sample an eclectic mix of dishes, from gourmet burgers and loaded fries to vegan tacos and artisanal doughnuts. The lively atmosphere, complete with live music and entertainment, makes it a popular destination for foodies and families alike.

The city's commitment to sustainability and local produce is evident in its thriving farmers' markets, where you can find fresh, seasonal ingredients from local producers. The Partick Farmers' Market, held twice a month, is a favorite among locals, offering a wide selection of organic vegetables, handmade cheeses, and freshly baked goods. Shopping at these markets provides an opportunity to support local farmers and artisans while discovering the best of Scotland's natural bounty.

For a more refined dining experience, Glasgow boasts a selection of award-winning restaurants that showcase the creativity and skill of its chefs. Cail Bruich, located in the West End, has earned critical acclaim for its innovative approach to Scottish cuisine. The menu, which changes with the seasons, features dishes that highlight the finest local ingredients, prepared with precision and flair. The restaurant's commitment to sustainability and ethical sourcing is reflected in every dish, creating a dining experience that is both memorable and meaningful.

Another standout is The Gannet, situated in the vibrant Finnieston area. This Michelin Bib Gourmand-awarded restaurant offers a contemporary take on Scottish cuisine, with a focus on bold flavors and inventive presentations. The menu, which changes regularly, showcases the best of Scotland's larder, from wild venison and Highland beef to foraged herbs and coastal vegetables. The Gannet's stylish yet relaxed setting provides the perfect backdrop for a memorable dining experience.

For a sweet treat, Glasgow's bakeries and patisseries offer a tempting array of confections. Tantrum Doughnuts, with locations in the West End and city center, is renowned for its artisanal doughnuts, made fresh daily using locally sourced ingredients. With flavors ranging from classic glazed to inventive creations like pistachio and hibiscus, these doughnuts are a must-try for anyone with a sweet tooth.

Glasgow's culinary scene is a testament to the city's creativity, diversity, and passion for good food. Whether you're indulging in traditional Scottish dishes, exploring global flavors, or savoring innovative creations, the city's culinary delights promise an unforgettable experience. As you navigate the bustling streets and vibrant neighborhoods, you'll discover a world of flavors waiting to be explored, each offering a taste of Glasgow's unique and dynamic spirit.

Nightlife and Entertainment

Glasgow, a city renowned for its vibrant and eclectic nightlife, offers an array of entertainment options that cater to diverse tastes and preferences. As the sun sets over the city, Glasgow comes alive with a buzz of activity, inviting locals and visitors alike to explore its dynamic offerings. From lively pubs and stylish cocktail bars to pulsating clubs and intimate music venues, the city's nightlife scene is nothing short of exhilarating.

The iconic West End is a popular starting point for an evening out. Known for its bohemian charm and bustling atmosphere, this area is home to a multitude of bars and pubs that offer a welcoming ambiance and a diverse selection of drinks. Ashton Lane, a cobbled street lined with fairy lights, is a favorite haunt for those seeking a cozy yet lively setting. Here, you'll find establishments like The Ubiquitous Chip, known for its extensive whisky selection and warm, rustic vibe. The Lane Bar, located within the same venue, offers a chic cocktail menu, perfect for those in search of a more refined experience.

For a taste of Glasgow's rich brewing tradition, head to one of the city's many craft beer bars. Shilling Brewing Co., situated in the city center, is a must-visit for beer enthusiasts. This bar and brewery offers a rotating selection of craft beers brewed on-site, along with a curated selection of guest ales. The relaxed and friendly atmosphere makes it an ideal spot for sampling local brews and enjoying a casual night out with friends.

As the night progresses, Glasgow's music scene takes center stage. The city is home to a plethora of live music venues, each offering a unique experience. King Tut's Wah Wah Hut, a legendary venue in the music world, continues to be a launching pad for emerging talent. With its intimate setting and electric atmosphere, King Tut's is the perfect place to discover the next big thing in music. The venue's storied history and commitment to showcasing new artists make it a must-visit for music lovers.

The Barrowland Ballroom, affectionately known as "The Barras," is another iconic venue that has hosted countless legendary performances. Known for its distinctive sprung dance floor and vibrant atmosphere, The Barras is a rite of passage for both bands and fans. With a lineup that includes rock, indie, and everything in between, this venue reflects the city's diverse musical tastes and energetic spirit.

For those seeking a more sophisticated musical experience, the Royal Concert Hall offers world-class performances in a grand setting. Home to the Royal Scottish National Orchestra, the hall hosts a variety of concerts, ranging from classical masterpieces to contemporary compositions. Its acoustics and grandeur make it a premier location for orchestral performances, providing an unforgettable evening of musical excellence.

Glasgow's club scene is equally dynamic, with venues offering everything from electronic beats to retro classics. Sub Club, located in the city center, is a legendary nightclub that has been at the forefront of Glasgow's electronic music scene for decades. Known for its cutting-edge sound system and innovative DJ lineups, Sub Club offers an immersive experience for dance music enthusiasts. The club's intimate setting and dedicated crowd create an atmosphere that is both electric and welcoming.

For a more eclectic clubbing experience, head to SWG3, a multi-purpose venue in the West End. This sprawling complex hosts a diverse range of events, from club nights and live gigs to art exhibitions and pop-up markets. With its industrial-chic aesthetic and ever-evolving program, SWG3 is a hub of creativity and nightlife, attracting a diverse crowd from across the city.

In addition to its bars, clubs, and music venues, Glasgow offers a wealth of entertainment options for those seeking a different kind of night out. The city's comedy scene is thriving, with venues like The Stand Comedy Club offering regular shows featuring both local talent and well-known comedians. The club's intimate setting and lively atmosphere make it a perfect spot for a night of laughter and entertainment.

For those interested in the performing arts, Glasgow's theaters provide a rich array of options. The Theatre Royal, home to the Scottish Opera and Scottish Ballet, offers a diverse program of performances, from classic operas and ballets to contemporary productions. The Citizens Theatre, known for its innovative approach to theater, presents a dynamic lineup of plays and performances that challenge and inspire.

Cinephiles will find plenty to enjoy at Glasgow's independent cinemas, which offer a curated selection of films in unique settings. The Glasgow Film Theatre, a beloved institution in the city, showcases an eclectic mix of independent, foreign, and classic films. Its retro charm and carefully selected programming make it a favorite among film enthusiasts. The Everyman Cinema, located in Princes Square, offers a luxurious movie-going experience, complete with plush seating and a gourmet menu.

Glasgow's nightlife and entertainment scene is a testament to the city's creativity, diversity, and passion for life. Whether you're sipping cocktails in a stylish bar, dancing the night away in a pulsating club, or enjoying a live performance in an iconic venue, the city's offerings promise an unforgettable experience. As you navigate Glasgow's vibrant streets and bustling neighborhoods, you'll discover a world of entertainment waiting to be explored, each offering a glimpse into the city's unique and dynamic spirit.

Day Trips from Glasgow

Glasgow, with its vibrant culture and dynamic energy, serves as an ideal base for exploring the natural beauty and historical richness of surrounding Scotland. The city's strategic location provides easy access to a variety of day trips, each offering unique landscapes, charming towns, and intriguing stories. As you set out on these excursions, the diversity of Scotland's scenery unfolds, from serene lochs and rugged highlands to quaint villages and historic sites.

Loch Lomond and The Trossachs National Park is one of the most accessible day trips from Glasgow, located just a short drive to the north. Known for its breathtaking scenery, the park is a haven for outdoor enthusiasts. Loch Lomond, the largest inland stretch of water in Great Britain by surface area, offers a stunning backdrop for activities such as hiking, kayaking, and sailing. The quaint village of Balloch, on the southern shores of the loch, serves as a gateway to the park. Here, the Loch Lomond Shores complex provides an array of shopping and dining options, as well as the Sea Life Aquarium, making it a perfect starting point for families.

For those seeking a more leisurely pace, a cruise on Loch Lomond offers a tranquil way to absorb the area's beauty. Several operators provide boat tours that glide past the loch's many islands, each steeped in local legend and lore. The picturesque village of Luss, with its charming cottages and floral displays, is a delightful stop along the loch's western shore. Its sandy beach and scenic pier provide stunning views of the surrounding hills, making it a favorite spot for both locals and visitors.

A journey eastwards brings you to the historic city of Stirling, where the past comes to life amidst its ancient streets and impressive landmarks. Stirling Castle, perched atop a volcanic rock, is a symbol of Scotland's rich history and a must-visit site. The castle has witnessed many significant events in Scottish history and offers an immersive experience with its well-preserved architecture, informative exhibits, and stunning views of the surrounding countryside. Nearby, the Wallace Monument stands as a tribute to Scotland's national hero, Sir William Wallace. The monument's tower provides panoramic views of the Ochil Hills and the city below, rewarding those who climb its spiral staircase with a breathtaking vista.

Venturing further afield, the coastal town of Ayr offers a delightful escape to Scotland's rugged western coast. Known for its sandy beaches and maritime heritage, Ayr is an ideal destination for a relaxing day by the sea. The historic Ayrshire coast is steeped in tales of seafaring and adventure, with sites such as the Robert Burns Birthplace Museum providing insights into the life and works of Scotland's beloved poet. Visitors can explore Burns Cottage, the poet's birthplace, and enjoy a stroll through the picturesque gardens that surround it.

Just a short distance from Ayr, Culzean Castle and Country Park presents an enchanting blend of history and nature. This grand castle, set amidst sprawling parklands, offers guided tours that delve into its storied past and architectural splendor. The surrounding grounds, with their lush gardens and woodland trails, invite exploration and provide a haven for wildlife. The dramatic cliffs and shoreline offer stunning views of the Firth of Clyde and beyond, creating a picturesque setting for a leisurely day out.

For those drawn to the mystique of Scotland's ancient past, a trip to the village of Callander opens the door to the Trossachs' rich history and folklore. Known as the "Gateway to the Highlands," Callander offers a charming blend of tradition and natural beauty. Visitors can explore the nearby Bracklinn Falls, a series of cascading waterfalls set within a lush forest, or embark on a hike to explore the surrounding hills and lochs that define the region's landscape.

The Isle of Arran, often referred to as "Scotland in miniature," is a captivating day trip for those seeking diverse landscapes and outdoor adventures. Accessible by ferry from Ardrossan, Arran offers a microcosm of Scotland's natural beauty, with its rugged mountains, serene beaches, and lush forests. The island's main village, Brodick, is home to Brodick Castle and Gardens, a historic estate set against the backdrop of Goat Fell, the island's highest peak. Visitors can explore the castle's opulent interiors and expansive gardens, or take on the challenge of hiking to the summit of Goat Fell for sweeping views of the surrounding islands and mainland.

For a more leisurely exploration, the island's coastal roads provide scenic drives that reveal secluded bays, charming villages, and inviting local eateries. The Arran Distillery offers tours and tastings, providing an opportunity to sample the island's renowned whisky and learn about the craft of distillation. With its diverse offerings, Arran is an ideal destination for both relaxation and adventure.

In the opposite direction, the picturesque town of Oban serves as a gateway to Scotland's western isles. Known as the "Seafood Capital of Scotland," Oban offers a delightful culinary experience with its fresh seafood and lively harbor.

Visitors can explore McCaig's Tower, an iconic structure that offers panoramic views of the town and the islands beyond. Oban's bustling waterfront is a departure point for ferries to the Isles of Mull, Iona, and Staffa, each offering its own unique attractions and landscapes.

The Isle of Mull, with its rugged coastline and abundant wildlife, invites exploration and discovery. The island's capital, Tobermory, is famous for its colorful waterfront and serves as a hub for island tours and wildlife excursions. Nearby, the Isle of Iona is renowned for its spiritual heritage and historic abbey, while the uninhabited Isle of Staffa is known for its striking basalt columns and the enchanting Fingal's Cave.

Glasgow's location provides easy access to a wealth of day trip destinations, each offering unique experiences and insights into Scotland's natural beauty and cultural heritage. Whether you're drawn to the tranquility of a loch, the history of an ancient castle, or the charm of a coastal village, these excursions promise a rich and rewarding exploration of Scotland's diverse landscapes. As you embark on these journeys, the stories and beauty of the Scottish countryside unfold, creating unforgettable memories and deepening your connection to this remarkable land.

CHAPTER 3: THE MAJESTIC HIGHLANDS

Scenic Drives and Routes

The Highlands of Scotland, a majestic landscape sculpted by nature's hand, offer some of the most breathtaking scenic drives and routes in the world. Each journey through this rugged terrain is a sensory feast, with vistas that range from towering mountains and tranquil lochs to verdant glens and windswept coasts. As you navigate these routes, the beauty and solitude of the Highlands invite reflection, adventure, and discovery.

One of the most iconic drives in the Highlands is the North Coast 500, a 516-mile loop that begins and ends in the city of Inverness. Dubbed Scotland's answer to Route 66, this route takes you through some of the most spectacular landscapes the country has to offer. As you set out from Inverness, the gateway to the Highlands, the road leads you along the rugged east coast toward the charming town of Wick. Here, the dramatic cliffs and seascapes set the tone for the journey ahead.

Continuing northward, the route passes through the historic town of Thurso before reaching John o' Groats, the northernmost point of mainland Britain. This iconic landmark offers stunning views across the Pentland Firth to the Orkney Islands, providing a perfect spot for a pause and a photo opportunity. From here, the road winds westward, hugging the coastline and revealing hidden bays, sweeping beaches, and secluded villages.

The drive through the dramatic landscapes of Sutherland and Wester Ross is a highlight of the North Coast 500. The jagged peaks of the Torridon Hills rise in the distance, their imposing presence a testament to the geological forces that shaped this land. The road meanders through Glen Torridon, where ancient mountains cradle the glen in a breathtaking embrace. As you navigate this route, the changing light creates a kaleidoscope of colors, transforming the scenery with every passing hour.

Further along the route, the village of Applecross beckons with its remote charm and stunning views across the Inner Sound to the Isle of Skye. To reach Applecross, you'll traverse the Bealach na Bà, a mountain pass that offers one of the most exhilarating drives in Scotland. This narrow, winding road climbs steeply to an elevation of 2,054 feet, rewarding those who brave its hairpin bends with panoramic vistas that stretch for miles. The descent into Applecross is equally dramatic, with the village's tranquil setting providing a stark contrast to the wild beauty of the pass.

For those seeking a more leisurely pace, the Road to the Isles offers a picturesque journey from Fort William to Mallaig. This 46-mile route takes you through the heart of the West Highlands, offering glimpses of some of Scotland's most iconic scenery. As you leave Fort William, the towering presence of Ben Nevis, the UK's highest peak, looms to the east. The road follows the shoreline of Loch Eil before winding through the picturesque Glenfinnan, where the famous viaduct spans the valley. Fans of the Harry Potter series will recognize this viaduct as the route of the Hogwarts Express, and the view from the nearby Glenfinnan Monument is simply magical.

Continuing westward, the road skirts the shores of Loch Shiel and Loch Morar, offering glimpses of their tranquil waters framed by rugged hills. The journey culminates in the bustling fishing port of Mallaig, where fresh seafood and ferry connections to the Isle of Skye await. The Road to the Isles is a celebration of the West Highlands' natural beauty, with each turn revealing a new and captivating vista.

The Cairngorms National Park, located in the eastern Highlands, offers another stunning backdrop for a scenic drive. The Snow Roads Scenic Route, a 90-mile journey through the park, showcases the rugged beauty and diverse landscapes of this region. Starting in the village of Blairgowrie, the route winds through rolling hills and moorland, passing through charming villages like Braemar and Ballater.

The Cairngorms' distinctive granite peaks dominate the skyline, their ancient forms shaped by millennia of glacial activity. As you drive, the landscape transitions from pastoral glens to wild, open moorland, with the opportunity to spot wildlife such as red deer and golden eagles. The route also offers access to some of Scotland's most renowned whisky distilleries, where you can savor the region's distinctive malts and learn about the craft of whisky-making.

The Isle of Skye, often referred to as the "Misty Isle," offers a dramatic and otherworldly landscape that is best explored by car. The Trotternish Loop, a 50-mile circuit on the island's northern peninsula, takes you through some of Skye's most iconic scenery. The route begins in the charming town of Portree, where colorful harbor buildings create a postcard-perfect scene.

As you leave Portree, the road leads you to the Old Man of Storr, a towering rock formation that rises starkly against the sky. This iconic landmark is a popular hiking destination, offering panoramic views of the surrounding landscape. Continuing along the loop, the Quiraing presents a surreal landscape of jagged peaks and hidden valleys, sculpted by ancient landslides. The drive through this otherworldly terrain is an awe-inspiring experience, with every turn revealing a new and breathtaking view.

Further along the route, the Kilt Rock and Mealt Falls offer a dramatic coastal vista, where basalt columns resembling a kilt cascade into the sea. The loop concludes with a visit to the Fairy Glen, a whimsical landscape of conical hills and mysterious rock formations that evoke the island's rich folklore.

The Highlands' scenic drives and routes offer an unparalleled opportunity to immerse yourself in the natural beauty and cultural heritage of this remarkable region. Whether you're navigating the winding roads of the North Coast 500, exploring the tranquil landscapes of the Cairngorms, or discovering the mystical allure of Skye, each journey promises a unique and unforgettable experience. As you traverse these routes, the majesty and mystery of the Highlands unfold, creating lasting memories and a deep appreciation for Scotland's wild and untamed beauty.

Hiking and Outdoor Adventures

The Highlands of Scotland, with their untamed beauty and rugged landscapes, present a paradise for outdoor enthusiasts and adventurers alike. This region, known for its towering peaks, expansive moorlands, and serene lochs, offers a myriad of opportunities for hiking and exploration. Each path and trail tells its own story, inviting you to step into a world where nature reigns supreme and adventure awaits at every turn.

One of the most iconic hiking experiences in the Highlands is conquering Ben Nevis, the UK's highest peak. Rising 1,345 meters above sea level, Ben Nevis attracts thousands of hikers each year, drawn by the challenge and the promise of breathtaking views from the summit. The most popular route, the Mountain Track (or Tourist Path), offers a well-trodden path to the top, taking approximately 7 to 9 hours for the round trip. As you ascend, the landscape shifts from lush meadows and heather-clad slopes to rocky terrain and scree, culminating in a summit that offers panoramic views of the surrounding mountains and glens. Preparedness is key, as weather conditions can change rapidly, so packing appropriate gear, including waterproofs and warm clothing, is essential.

For those seeking solitude and a connection with nature, the West Highland Way presents an unforgettable long-distance hiking experience. Spanning 96 miles from Milngavie, near Glasgow, to Fort William, this trail weaves through some of Scotland's most stunning landscapes. The route takes you along the shores of Loch Lomond, through the rugged expanse of Rannoch Moor, and into the heart of Glen Coe, each section revealing a new facet of the Highlands' character. The trail can be completed in stages or tackled in its entirety over a week, with accommodations ranging from campsites and hostels to cozy inns and B&Bs along the way. The camaraderie among fellow hikers and the ever-changing scenery make this journey a truly rewarding adventure.

For a hike that combines history with natural beauty, the Great Glen Way offers a fascinating exploration of Scotland's geological and cultural heritage. Stretching 79 miles from Fort William to Inverness, this route follows the Great Glen Fault, a natural fissure that divides the Highlands into the Grampian Mountains and the Northwest Highlands. The trail takes you along the banks of the Caledonian Canal and past the iconic waters of Loch Ness, with opportunities to spot the elusive Loch Ness Monster. The varied terrain, which includes forest tracks, canal towpaths, and open moorland, provides a diverse hiking experience, with each section offering its own unique challenges and rewards.

For those looking to explore the Highlands' lesser-known gems, the Isle of Skye offers a wealth of hiking opportunities amid its dramatic landscapes. The Quiraing, located on the Trotternish Peninsula, is a geological wonder that offers a moderate hike through a surreal landscape of towering pinnacles and hidden valleys. The circuit, which takes around 2 to 3 hours to complete, offers stunning views of the surrounding sea and islands, as well as the chance to explore the unique rock formations that make this area so distinctive.

The Cuillin Ridge, also on Skye, presents a more challenging adventure for experienced hikers and climbers. This jagged range of peaks is renowned for its technical difficulty and offers some of the most exhilarating mountaineering experiences in the UK. The traverse of the main ridge is a serious undertaking, requiring rock climbing skills and a head for heights, but the rewards are immense, with unrivaled views and a sense of accomplishment that comes from conquering one of Scotland's most formidable landscapes.

The Cairngorms National Park, located in the eastern Highlands, offers a different kind of adventure, with its vast plateaus and ancient forests providing a haven for wildlife and outdoor activities. Hiking in the Cairngorms offers the chance to explore the park's unique ecosystems, from the arctic-like tundra of the high peaks to the ancient Caledonian pine forests that shelter a rich diversity of flora and fauna. The Lairig Ghru, a mountain pass that cuts through the heart of the Cairngorms, offers a challenging hike through a landscape of glacial valleys and towering cliffs. This 19-mile route is best tackled over two days, with an overnight camp or stay in a bothy, providing a true wilderness experience.

For a more leisurely exploration, the Rothiemurchus Estate offers a network of trails through its ancient woodlands, providing opportunities for wildlife watching and photography. The estate is home to red squirrels, capercaillie, and a variety of bird species, making it a paradise for nature lovers. The Loch an Eilein trail, a 4-mile circuit around a picturesque loch with a ruined castle on an island, offers a gentle walk with plenty of opportunities to soak in the serene beauty of the surroundings.

Beyond hiking, the Highlands offer a wealth of outdoor adventures for those seeking to explore the region's diverse landscapes. Kayaking and canoeing on the lochs and rivers provide a unique perspective on the scenery, with the chance to explore hidden coves and remote beaches. The River Spey, with its gentle flow and stunning backdrop, offers an ideal setting for a multi-day canoe trip, with the opportunity to camp along the riverbanks and enjoy the tranquility of the Highlands.

For adrenaline seekers, the Highlands offer a range of thrilling activities, from mountain biking on rugged trails to rock climbing on towering cliffs. The Nevis Range, near Fort William, offers world-class mountain biking trails, with routes ranging from gentle forest tracks to challenging downhill courses. The area's natural terrain, combined with purpose-built trails, provides an exhilarating experience for riders of all abilities.

Rock climbing enthusiasts will find plenty of challenges among the crags and cliffs of the Highlands, with classic routes such as the Old Man of Stoer and the sea cliffs of Reiff offering a mix of traditional and sport climbing opportunities. The region's diverse geology provides a variety of climbing experiences, from granite slabs and basalt columns to sandstone towers, each offering its own unique challenges and rewards.

The Highlands of Scotland, with their awe-inspiring landscapes and endless opportunities for exploration, offer a playground for adventurers and nature lovers alike. Whether you're hiking through ancient glens, paddling along serene lochs, or scaling rugged peaks, the Highlands promise an unforgettable journey into the heart of Scotland's wild beauty. As you embark on these adventures, the spirit of the land and its stories will leave an indelible mark, creating memories that will last a lifetime.

Iconic Castles and Historical Sites

The Highlands of Scotland are steeped in history, their landscapes dotted with iconic castles and ancient sites that whisper tales of the past. These structures, standing as testaments to Scotland's storied history, offer a glimpse into the lives of those who inhabited them and the events that shaped the region. Each castle and historical site carries its own unique narrative, inviting visitors to step back in time and explore the rich tapestry of the Highlands' heritage.

Eilean Donan Castle, arguably one of the most photographed castles in the world, is a symbol of the Highlands' romantic allure. Situated on a small tidal island where three lochs meet, Eilean Donan's picturesque setting and striking architecture make it a must-visit destination. The castle's origins date back to the 13th century, when it was built to defend against Viking invasions. Over the centuries, it has witnessed numerous battles and sieges, each leaving its mark on the structure. Today, Eilean Donan is meticulously restored, offering visitors the chance to explore its atmospheric rooms and learn about its storied past through informative exhibits and displays.

Moving eastward, the imposing ruins of Urquhart Castle stand sentinel on the shores of Loch Ness. This strategic site has been a focal point of Scottish history for over a thousand years, with its origins rooted in the early medieval period. The castle's turbulent history is mirrored in its weathered stones, which have borne witness to clan rivalries, sieges, and the relentless march of time. As you wander through the ruins, the breathtaking views of Loch Ness and the surrounding hills provide a dramatic backdrop to the castle's rich history. The visitor center offers insights into the castle's past, with multimedia presentations and artifacts that bring its stories to life.

In the heart of the Cairngorms National Park lies Balmoral Castle, a beloved residence of the British royal family. Purchased by Queen Victoria and Prince Albert in the 19th century, Balmoral is a symbol of the royal family's enduring connection to Scotland. The castle's stunning architecture, set against the backdrop of the Cairngorm Mountains, reflects the romantic vision of Prince Albert, who played a key role in its design. While the castle's interior remains private, visitors can explore the extensive grounds and gardens, which offer a glimpse into the life of the royal family and the natural beauty that surrounds this iconic estate.

Cawdor Castle, located near Inverness, is another gem of the Highlands, renowned for its enchanting gardens and literary connections. Immortalized by Shakespeare in "Macbeth," Cawdor Castle's history is intertwined with legend and lore. The castle's origins can be traced back to the 14th century, and it has been the home of the Cawdor family for over 600 years. Visitors can explore the castle's beautifully preserved rooms, which are filled with fine art, antiques, and tapestries. The surrounding gardens, with their vibrant displays of flowers and meticulously maintained grounds, provide a tranquil setting for a leisurely stroll.

Dunrobin Castle, perched on the east coast near Golspie, is the largest castle in the Northern Highlands and a striking example of Scottish baronial architecture. With its fairytale turrets and sweeping views of the North Sea, Dunrobin exudes a sense of grandeur and elegance. The castle has been home to the Earls and Dukes of Sutherland for over seven centuries, and its opulent interiors reflect the wealth and influence of its past occupants. Visitors can explore the castle's lavish rooms, as well as the formal gardens, which were inspired by the gardens of the Palace of Versailles. The gardens host regular falconry displays, offering an engaging glimpse into the ancient art of hunting with birds of prey.

A journey through the Highlands' historical sites would be incomplete without a visit to the ancient standing stones of Clava Cairns. Located near Inverness, this prehistoric burial site dates back over 4,000 years and offers a fascinating insight into the region's early inhabitants. The site comprises a series of stone circles and burial cairns, each with its own unique alignment and purpose. The atmospheric setting, surrounded by woodland and the gentle sound of the River Nairn, creates a sense of mystery and wonder. Clava Cairns is believed to have inspired the fictional Craigh na Dun in the "Outlander" series, adding an additional layer of intrigue for fans of the books and television show.

Further south, the ruins of Kilchurn Castle stand on the shores of Loch Awe, their haunting beauty captivating all who visit. Built in the mid-15th century by the Campbells of Glenorchy, the castle's strategic location made it a key stronghold in the region. Despite its ruinous state, Kilchurn's grandeur is evident in its imposing towers and sweeping views of the surrounding landscape. The loch and mountains provide a dramatic backdrop, creating a scene that is both serene and awe-inspiring. Kilchurn Castle is a photographer's dream, with its picturesque reflection in the loch offering countless opportunities to capture the essence of the Highlands.

As you venture deeper into the Highlands, the remnants of Castle Tioram emerge from the waters of Loch Moidart. This once-mighty fortress, built in the 13th century, is steeped in history and legend. Its remote location and atmospheric ruins evoke a sense of mystery, capturing the imagination of all who visit. Castle Tioram was the ancestral home of the Clanranald branch of Clan Donald, and its history is marked by clan battles and shifting allegiances. The castle's evocative ruins, set against the backdrop of the loch and surrounding hills, provide a hauntingly beautiful setting for exploration.

The Highlands' iconic castles and historical sites offer a journey through time, each revealing a chapter of Scotland's rich and complex history. From the romantic allure of Eilean Donan and the haunting beauty of Urquhart to the grandeur of Dunrobin and the mystery of Clava Cairns, these sites invite exploration and discovery. As you wander through their storied halls and atmospheric ruins, the echoes of the past come alive, weaving a tapestry of history, legend, and culture that is uniquely Scottish. The Highlands' landscape, with its rugged beauty and timeless charm, serves as the perfect canvas for these stories, creating an unforgettable experience that lingers long after your visit.

Wildlife and Nature Exploration

The Highlands of Scotland, with their vast and varied landscapes, offer a sanctuary for an abundance of wildlife and an ideal setting for nature exploration. From the rugged peaks of the Cairngorms to the serene shores of remote lochs, this region is a haven for those seeking to connect with the natural world. Each corner of the Highlands presents unique ecosystems and habitats, inviting visitors to uncover the secrets of its flora and fauna.

One of the most distinctive features of the Highlands is its diverse wildlife, which thrives in the region's varied climates and terrains. The iconic red deer, often seen as a symbol of the Scottish wilderness, roams the hills and glens. These majestic creatures, with their impressive antlers and regal bearing, are most easily spotted during the autumn rutting season, when stags compete for dominance. Guided wildlife tours provide an excellent opportunity to observe these animals in their natural habitat, offering insights into their behavior and the challenges they face.

The elusive golden eagle, a master of the skies, is another emblematic species of the Highlands. With its impressive wingspan and keen eyesight, this apex predator soars above the mountains and moorlands, hunting for its next meal. Birdwatchers and nature enthusiasts flock to the Highlands to catch a glimpse of this magnificent bird, often venturing to remote areas where they are more commonly found. The hills and cliffs of the Cairngorms and the Isle of Skye provide prime locations for eagle spotting, with guided tours and observation points enhancing the experience.

On the coastal fringes of the Highlands, marine life flourishes in the nutrient-rich waters. The Moray Firth, a large inlet of the North Sea, is home to a resident population of bottlenose dolphins. These intelligent and playful creatures are often seen frolicking in the waves, delighting observers with their acrobatic displays. Boat tours offer a thrilling way to encounter these dolphins up close, with knowledgeable guides providing information about their behavior and conservation efforts. Alongside dolphins, the waters of the Highlands support a variety of other marine life, including seals, porpoises, and occasionally even whales.

The Highlands' rivers and lochs are teeming with life, providing vital habitats for a range of species. The Atlantic salmon, an iconic fish of Scottish rivers, embarks on an extraordinary journey from the ocean to its freshwater spawning grounds. Witnessing the salmon leap upstream is a remarkable sight, with the rivers of the Highlands offering several locations to observe this natural spectacle. Fishing enthusiasts can also enjoy angling in these waters, though sustainable practices and respect for local regulations are essential to preserving the delicate balance of these ecosystems.

The ancient Caledonian pine forests, remnants of a once-vast woodland that covered much of Scotland, offer a glimpse into the Highlands' ecological history. These forests, home to a rich diversity of species, provide a tranquil setting for exploration and discovery. Among the towering Scots pines and lush undergrowth, you may encounter the red squirrel, a charming and endangered species that thrives in these wooded environments. The forests also host a variety of birdlife, including the capercaillie, a large and elusive grouse that requires careful stewardship to ensure its survival.

The Cairngorms National Park, one of the UK's most significant protected areas, offers a wealth of opportunities for nature exploration and wildlife observation. The park's diverse landscapes, from high mountains to ancient woodlands, support a wide range of species. Guided walks and ranger-led activities provide valuable insights into the park's ecosystems and the conservation efforts underway to preserve them. The Cairngorms are also home to the rare Scottish wildcat, a species that faces numerous threats but remains a symbol of the wild heart of Scotland.

For those interested in botany, the Highlands' flora is as varied and fascinating as its fauna. The region's unique climate and geology support a wealth of plant life, from hardy alpine species clinging to the mountainsides to delicate wildflowers carpeting the meadows. The machair, a rare coastal habitat found on the western fringes of the Highlands, is a botanist's dream, with its vibrant display of wildflowers supporting a rich diversity of insect life. This habitat, characterized by its sandy soil and proximity to the sea, is a vital breeding ground for birds such as the corncrake and the lapwing.

Exploring the Highlands' nature often involves venturing into remote and wild areas, where the rewards are rich but the conditions can be challenging. Proper preparation and respect for the environment are essential for a safe and enjoyable experience. Wearing appropriate clothing and footwear, carrying sufficient supplies, and being aware of changing weather conditions are crucial when exploring the Highlands' rugged terrain. Additionally, understanding and adhering to the Scottish Outdoor Access Code ensures that the natural beauty of the region is preserved for future generations.

The Highlands also offer a range of visitor centers and nature reserves, providing educational resources and opportunities to learn more about the region's wildlife and conservation efforts. These centers, often staffed by knowledgeable guides and rangers, offer exhibits, guided walks, and talks that deepen your understanding of the local ecosystems and the challenges they face. Engaging with these resources enhances your appreciation of the Highlands and inspires a deeper connection to the natural world.

In the Highlands, each exploration is an invitation to discover the wonders of Scotland's wild heart. The region's diverse landscapes and rich biodiversity offer endless opportunities for adventure and discovery, whether you're observing the majestic flight of a golden eagle, tracing the path of a salmon upstream, or simply enjoying the tranquility of a pristine loch. As you immerse yourself in the natural beauty of the Highlands, the stories of the land and its inhabitants unfold, revealing the intricate web of life that defines this extraordinary region. Each encounter with the wild fosters a deeper appreciation for the delicate balance of nature and the importance of preserving these landscapes for generations to come.

Local Traditions and Festivals

The Highlands of Scotland, a land of breathtaking landscapes and rich cultural heritage, are steeped in traditions and festivals that offer a window into the soul of this unique region. These events, rooted in history and community, celebrate the customs, music, and stories that have been passed down through generations. For those who visit, participating in local traditions and festivals provides an opportunity to engage with the Highland spirit and experience the vibrancy of its cultural life.

One of the most iconic and enduring traditions in the Highlands is the Highland Games. These events, held annually in various towns and villages, showcase feats of strength, skill, and endurance, reflecting the martial heritage of the Scottish clans. The Games typically feature events such as the caber toss, hammer throw, and tug-of-war, each demanding exceptional physical prowess. Competitors, often clad in traditional kilts, vie for glory as spectators cheer them on. Beyond the athletic contests, the Highland Games also celebrate Scottish music and dance, with pipe bands, Highland dancing, and ceilidhs adding to the festive atmosphere. The Braemar Gathering, held in the village of Braemar, is one of the most famous of these events, attracting thousands of visitors and even members of the British royal family.

The Highlands are also home to a rich musical tradition, with folk music playing a central role in the region's cultural life. One of the most celebrated events is the Hebridean Celtic Festival, held on the Isle of Lewis. This festival brings together musicians from across Scotland and beyond, showcasing a diverse range of traditional and contemporary Celtic music. The festival's vibrant atmosphere, set against the stunning backdrop of the Outer Hebrides, creates an unforgettable experience for music lovers. Visitors can immerse themselves in the sounds of fiddles, bagpipes, and Gaelic song, enjoying performances from both established artists and emerging talents.

Gaelic culture, integral to the identity of the Highlands, is celebrated through various festivals and events that highlight the region's linguistic and cultural heritage. The Royal National Mòd, Scotland's premier Gaelic cultural festival, is a week-long celebration of Gaelic language, music, and arts. Held in different locations each year, the Mòd features competitions in singing, poetry, drama, and storytelling, attracting participants and audiences from across the Gaelic-speaking world. The festival not only showcases the richness of Gaelic culture but also promotes its preservation and revitalization, fostering a deep sense of pride and identity among attendees.

Another cherished tradition in the Highlands is the ancient practice of storytelling, which has been a vital part of the region's cultural fabric for centuries. Storytelling festivals, such as the Scottish International Storytelling Festival, bring together storytellers from across the globe to share tales that entertain, educate, and inspire. These events celebrate the art of oral storytelling, a tradition that has long been used to pass down history, folklore, and moral lessons. In the intimate setting of a storytelling session, listeners are transported to a world of imagination, where legends of warriors, mythical creatures, and historical figures come to life.

The Highlands also celebrate their culinary heritage through various food and drink festivals that highlight the region's bountiful produce and traditional cuisine. The Highland Food and Drink Festival, for instance, showcases local artisans and producers, offering visitors a taste of the region's finest fare. From smoked salmon and venison to whisky and craft beer, the festival provides an opportunity to indulge in the flavors of the Highlands while learning about the region's culinary customs. Cooking demonstrations, tastings, and workshops add to the festival's appeal, allowing visitors to engage with the local food culture in a meaningful way.

Seasonal festivals, deeply rooted in the agricultural calendar, are another important aspect of Highland life. The Beltane Fire Festival, inspired by ancient Celtic traditions, marks the arrival of summer with a vibrant celebration of fire, music, and dance. Held annually in Edinburgh, the festival features a procession of performers and drummers, culminating in a spectacular bonfire on Calton Hill. Though not exclusively a Highland event, Beltane reflects the deep connection between the people of Scotland and the natural cycles of the earth, a bond that has been celebrated for centuries.

The Highland region also plays host to a variety of local fairs and gatherings, each with its own unique character and charm. These events, often centered around market towns, offer a glimpse into rural life and the strong sense of community that defines the Highlands. The Dornoch Highland Gathering, for example, combines traditional sports with a lively market, showcasing local crafts, produce, and entertainment. Such gatherings provide an opportunity for locals and visitors alike to come together, fostering a sense of camaraderie and shared heritage.

Throughout the year, the Highlands are alive with celebrations that honor the region's history, culture, and traditions. From the spirited competitions of the Highland Games to the haunting melodies of Gaelic song, these events offer a rich tapestry of experiences for those who seek to connect with the heart of the Highlands. Participating in these festivals not only provides insight into the customs and values of the region but also creates lasting memories and a deeper appreciation for the enduring spirit of the Scottish Highlands. As visitors engage with these vibrant traditions, they become part of a living heritage that continues to inspire and captivate all who encounter it.

Where to Stay in the Highlands

Finding the perfect place to stay in the Highlands is as much a part of the adventure as exploring its breathtaking landscapes and rich cultural heritage. The region offers a diverse range of accommodations, each providing a unique experience that complements the spirit of the Highlands. Whether you seek the rustic charm of a countryside cottage, the luxury of a historic castle hotel, or the camaraderie of a bustling hostel, the Highlands cater to every taste and budget.

For those who dream of living like royalty, the Highlands boast an array of castle hotels that offer a taste of opulence and history. These grand estates, set amid rolling hills and lochs, provide an unforgettable backdrop for your Highland experience. Inverlochy Castle Hotel, located near Fort William, is one such example. This 19th-century castle, nestled at the foot of Ben Nevis, offers sumptuous accommodations and fine dining, with each room beautifully appointed to reflect its storied past. Guests can partake in a range of activities, from fishing and clay pigeon shooting to leisurely strolls through the castle's extensive grounds.

For a more intimate encounter with the Highlands' storied past, consider staying in a historic inn or bed and breakfast. These charming establishments, often family-run, offer a warm welcome and personal touch that larger hotels may lack. Many of these inns are housed in buildings that date back centuries, providing a unique window into the region's history. The Old Inn at Gairloch, for instance, is a traditional Highland inn that exudes character and charm. With its cozy rooms, hearty meals, and stunning views over Loch Gairloch, it offers a quintessentially Scottish experience.

Those seeking a closer connection to nature will find an abundance of options in the Highlands' numerous self-catering cottages and cabins. These accommodations, ranging from rustic bothies to modern lodges, provide the freedom to explore the surrounding landscape at your own pace. A stay in a remote cottage allows you to experience the tranquility of the Highlands, with opportunities for hiking, wildlife watching, and stargazing right on your doorstep. Many of these properties are located in areas of outstanding natural beauty, such as the Cairngorms National Park or the Isle of Skye, offering unparalleled access to the region's stunning scenery.

For travelers on a budget or those seeking a more social experience, hostels and bunkhouses provide an affordable and convivial option. The Highlands are home to a network of hostels that cater to hikers, cyclists, and outdoor enthusiasts, offering a comfortable bed and the chance to share stories with fellow travelers. Hostels like the Loch Ossian Youth Hostel, set in a remote location accessible only by foot or train, offer a unique opportunity to disconnect from the hustle and bustle of modern life and immerse yourself in the natural beauty of the Highlands.

For a truly unique experience, consider staying in one of the Highlands' eco-friendly accommodations. These establishments, often situated in remote and pristine locations, prioritize sustainability and conservation, offering an opportunity to enjoy the region's natural beauty with minimal impact on the environment. The eco-lodges at the Alladale Wilderness Reserve, for example, provide a luxurious and sustainable retreat in the heart of the Highlands. Guests can participate in conservation activities, such as tree planting and wildlife monitoring, while enjoying the comfort and hospitality of the lodge.

Camping and caravanning offer yet another way to experience the Highlands, allowing you to stay close to nature and enjoy the freedom of the open road. The region boasts a wealth of campsites, from basic pitches in remote glens to well-equipped caravan parks with modern amenities. Wild camping, while more adventurous, is also an option, provided you adhere to the Scottish Outdoor Access Code and respect the environment. This approach allows you to experience the Highlands' rugged beauty firsthand, with the opportunity to wake up to the sight of mist-covered mountains or the sound of waves lapping against a loch.

For those traveling with families, the Highlands offer a range of family-friendly accommodations that cater to the needs of children and adults alike. Many hotels and lodges provide family rooms, play areas, and activities tailored to younger guests, ensuring a comfortable and enjoyable stay for all. The Macdonald Aviemore Resort, located in the Cairngorms, is a prime example, offering a range of facilities and entertainment options for families, including a swimming pool, soft play area, and outdoor adventure park.

In the Highlands, the choice of where to stay is as diverse as the landscape itself, offering a range of experiences that cater to different tastes and preferences. Whether you seek the grandeur of a castle hotel, the coziness of a country inn, or the serenity of a remote cottage, the Highlands have something to offer every traveler. Each accommodation provides a unique opportunity to connect with the region's natural beauty and rich cultural heritage, creating memories that will last a lifetime. As you plan your Highland adventure, consider the type of experience you wish to have and choose a place to stay that aligns with your vision, ensuring a truly unforgettable journey into the heart of Scotland's wild and enchanting landscape.

CHAPTER 4: THE ENCHANTING ISLES

Exploring the Isle of Skye

The Isle of Skye, the largest of the Inner Hebrides, is a land of dramatic landscapes and timeless beauty, where rugged mountains meet the sea in a symphony of natural splendor. This enchanting island, with its rich history and vibrant culture, beckons travelers to explore its many wonders, offering an experience that captures the essence of Scotland's wild heart.

Skye's allure begins with its breathtaking landscapes, each more awe-inspiring than the last. The Cuillin Hills, a range of jagged peaks and ridges, dominate the island's skyline, offering a paradise for hikers and climbers. These mountains, often shrouded in mist, provide a challenging and rewarding adventure for those who seek to conquer their summits. The Black Cuillin, with its dramatic cliffs and rocky terrain, presents a particularly demanding climb, while the Red Cuillin offers a gentler ascent with equally stunning views. For those less inclined to tackle the heights, the Quiraing, a unique landslip on the northern Trotternish Peninsula, offers an otherworldly landscape of pinnacles, plateaus, and hidden valleys, perfect for a leisurely walk or a more strenuous hike.

Alongside its towering mountains, Skye is famed for its picturesque coastal scenery and pristine beaches. The island's rugged coastline is punctuated by dramatic cliffs, sea stacks, and secluded coves, each offering a unique perspective on the island's natural beauty. Neist Point, a striking headland on Skye's westernmost tip, is one of the most iconic coastal landmarks. Here, the Neist Point Lighthouse stands sentinel against the Atlantic Ocean, providing a perfect vantage point for spotting dolphins, whales, and seabirds. Meanwhile, the coral sands of Claigan, near Dunvegan, offer a tranquil retreat, with turquoise waters and white sands reminiscent of more tropical climes.

Skye's rich tapestry of history is woven into its landscape, with ancient sites and ruins scattered across the island. The iconic Dunvegan Castle, the ancestral home of the Clan MacLeod, stands proudly on the shores of Loch Dunvegan. As the oldest continuously inhabited castle in Scotland, Dunvegan offers a fascinating glimpse into the island's past, with its impressive collection of artifacts and beautifully maintained gardens. Visitors can also embark on a boat trip from the castle to see the nearby seal colony, adding an element of wildlife exploration to their historical journey.

The island's Neolithic past is revealed in the standing stones and burial cairns that dot the landscape. The Fairy Glen, a whimsical and enchanting area near Uig, is a prime example of Skye's mystical allure. With its cone-shaped hills, grassy mounds, and labyrinthine paths, the Fairy Glen feels like a place where the lines between reality and legend blur. Equally captivating are the ancient brochs, such as Dun Beag and Dun Fiadhairt, which offer a tantalizing glimpse into the lives of Skye's early inhabitants.

The Isle of Skye is also a haven for wildlife enthusiasts, with its diverse habitats supporting a rich array of species. The island's coastal waters are home to otters, seals, and porpoises, while its moorlands provide a refuge for red deer and a variety of birdlife. The rare white-tailed sea eagle, with its impressive wingspan, can often be seen soaring above the island's cliffs and lochs. Guided wildlife tours offer the chance to explore Skye's natural habitats and observe its inhabitants, providing insights into the island's unique ecosystem and conservation efforts.

Skye's cultural heritage is as vibrant as its landscapes, with a thriving arts scene and a strong Gaelic tradition. The island is home to a number of galleries and craft studios, showcasing the work of local artists and artisans who draw inspiration from Skye's natural beauty. The Aros Centre in Portree, Skye's main town, offers a cultural hub where visitors can enjoy exhibitions, performances, and film screenings that celebrate the island's artistic and cultural life.

The Gaelic language, integral to Skye's identity, is celebrated through music, song, and storytelling. Traditional music sessions, or ceilidhs, can be found in local pubs and community halls, where visitors are welcome to join in the festivities. These gatherings provide an opportunity to experience the warmth and hospitality of the island's people, as well as the chance to learn a few Gaelic phrases and songs.

Skye's culinary scene is another highlight, with a focus on fresh, locally sourced ingredients that reflect the island's natural bounty. From seafood caught in the surrounding waters to venison and lamb reared on Skye's hills, the island's restaurants and eateries offer a true taste of the Highlands. The Michelin-starred Three Chimneys, located on the shores of Loch Dunvegan, is renowned for its innovative approach to traditional Scottish cuisine, while smaller cafes and bistros provide a more casual dining experience without compromising on quality.

Exploring the Isle of Skye is a journey of discovery, where each turn reveals a new facet of the island's beauty and character. Whether you choose to hike its mountains, wander its ancient sites, or immerse yourself in its cultural life, Skye offers an experience that is both enriching and exhilarating. The island's landscapes, steeped in history and legend, provide a backdrop for adventures that linger long in the memory, inviting you to return and uncover even more of its secrets. As you explore Skye, you become part of its story, contributing to the tapestry of experiences that define this extraordinary island.

Hidden Gems of the Orkney Islands

The Orkney Islands, an archipelago off the northern coast of Scotland, are a treasure trove of hidden gems waiting to be discovered. While the islands are known for their dramatic landscapes and ancient history, there are countless lesser-known sites and experiences that offer a deeper understanding of Orkney's unique character. From secluded beaches to mysterious archaeological sites, these hidden gems invite visitors to explore beyond the usual tourist paths.

One of Orkney's most captivating secrets is the island of Rousay, often referred to as the "Egypt of the North" due to its rich concentration of archaeological sites. Rousay is home to over 160 ancient monuments, including chambered cairns, brochs, and standing stones, all set against a backdrop of stunning coastal scenery. The Midhowe Broch and Cairn, perched on the edge of Eynhallow Sound, offer a fascinating insight into the island's prehistoric past. The cairn, a large stone burial chamber, is particularly impressive, with its intricately constructed interior and the atmospheric setting that transports visitors back in time.

Another hidden gem on Rousay is the Trumland Estate, a historic house and gardens that provide a glimpse into Orkney's more recent history. The estate, designed by the renowned architect David Bryce in the 19th century, features beautiful gardens and woodlands that contrast with the island's rugged landscape. Visitors can enjoy a leisurely walk through the grounds, taking in the diverse plant life and the tranquil atmosphere.

Orkney's natural wonders extend to its coastline, where secluded beaches and dramatic cliffs offer breathtaking views and opportunities for exploration. Rackwick Beach on the island of Hoy is one such hidden gem, known for its striking red sandstone cliffs and golden sands framed by rolling hills. The beach is a haven for wildlife, with seals and seabirds often spotted along the shore. Reaching Rackwick involves a scenic walk through the rugged landscape, culminating in the reward of this serene and untouched coastal paradise.

For those interested in Orkney's maritime heritage, the island of Shapinsay offers a unique glimpse into the past at the Balfour Castle and Gardens. Built in the 19th century, the castle is a fine example of Scottish baronial architecture, set within beautifully landscaped gardens. While the castle itself is not open to the public, visitors can explore the gardens and enjoy the stunning views across the surrounding islands. The island's coastal path is also worth exploring, offering the chance to discover hidden coves and dramatic sea views.

Orkney's hidden gems extend beneath the waves, with the islands offering some of the best diving opportunities in the UK. Scapa Flow, a natural harbor sheltered by the Orkney archipelago, is renowned for its shipwrecks, which attract divers from around the world. The wrecks, remnants of the German High Seas Fleet scuttled at the end of World War I, provide a fascinating underwater playground for experienced divers. The crystal-clear waters and abundance of marine life make Scapa Flow a must-visit destination for those with a passion for diving and maritime history.

For a truly off-the-beaten-path experience, the island of Papa Westray, affectionately known as Papay, offers a unique blend of history, wildlife, and community spirit. Despite its small size, Papay is home to a wealth of archaeological sites, including the Knap of Howar, the oldest known stone house in northern Europe. The island's rich birdlife, including puffins, arctic terns, and skuas, draws birdwatchers and nature enthusiasts alike. Visitors can also immerse themselves in the island's vibrant community, with local events and festivals providing an opportunity to engage with Papay's welcoming residents.

Orkney's hidden gems are not limited to its landscapes and history; the islands also boast a thriving arts scene, with many local artists drawing inspiration from their surroundings. The Pier Arts Centre in Stromness is a hidden cultural gem, showcasing contemporary art in a beautifully restored building overlooking the harbor. The center's collection includes works by renowned artists such as Barbara Hepworth and Ben Nicholson, alongside pieces by local Orkney artists. The gallery's location, with its stunning views and tranquil ambiance, makes it a perfect spot to reflect and appreciate the connection between art and nature.

The islands' culinary offerings also provide a taste of Orkney's hidden treasures, with local produce and traditional dishes reflecting the region's unique flavors. The Orkney Islands are renowned for their seafood, with fresh lobster, crab, and scallops featuring prominently on menus. Local delicacies such as Orkney cheese, bere bannocks, and Highland Park whisky offer a true taste of the islands, with many restaurants and cafes showcasing these ingredients in their dishes. Visitors can also explore Orkney's food and drink scene through farm tours and tastings, providing an opportunity to learn about the islands' culinary heritage and sustainable practices.

While Orkney's famous sites such as Skara Brae and the Ring of Brodgar are not to be missed, the islands' hidden gems offer an equally rewarding experience for those willing to venture off the beaten path. Whether you're exploring the ancient monuments of Rousay, diving into the depths of Scapa Flow, or savoring the flavors of Orkney's larder, these lesser-known attractions provide a deeper connection to the islands' rich tapestry of history, culture, and natural beauty. Each hidden gem invites you to uncover a new facet of Orkney, creating memories and experiences that will linger long after your visit has ended.

Distilleries and Whisky Tours

The allure of the Scottish Isles is not complete without indulging in one of Scotland's most iconic exports—whisky. The Isles, with their unique landscapes and climate, produce some of the most distinctive and celebrated whiskies in the world. From the peaty, smoky flavors of Islay to the maritime notes of the Hebrides, each isle offers a unique take on this storied spirit. Embarking on a journey through the distilleries of the Isles not only provides a sensory experience of the whisky itself but also offers a deep dive into the rich history and culture that surrounds it.

Islay, often referred to as "Whisky Island," is a must-visit for any whisky enthusiast. The island is home to nine working distilleries, each with its own character and flavor profile. Laphroaig, known for its intensely peaty and medicinal flavor, offers tours that take visitors through the entire production process, from malting the barley to the final maturation. The distillery's location, set against the rugged coastline, provides a stunning backdrop as you sample their iconic whiskies.

A visit to Ardbeg Distillery offers not only a chance to taste one of Islay's peatiest whiskies but also a glimpse into the innovative practices that have kept this distillery at the forefront of whisky production. The Ardbeg tour includes a walk through the distillery's traditional processes, as well as an opportunity to taste some of their experimental cask finishes, providing a comprehensive understanding of what makes Islay whisky so unique.

Islay's Bowmore Distillery, one of Scotland's oldest distilleries, offers a contrasting experience with its balance of peat and fruitiness. The Bowmore tour includes a visit to the famed No. 1 Vaults, the oldest maturation warehouse in Scotland, where you can witness the effect of time and sea air on whisky aging. The tour concludes with a tasting of Bowmore's distinctive range, allowing you to appreciate the subtleties in their flavor profiles.

Moving north, the Isle of Skye is home to the renowned Talisker Distillery, the oldest working distillery on the island. Talisker's whisky is known for its maritime character, reflecting the island's windswept shores. A tour of Talisker provides insight into the island's influence on whisky production, from the use of peated malt to the effect of the Atlantic on the aging process. The tour culminates in a tasting session that highlights the bold and complex flavors of Talisker's expressions.

The Isle of Jura, a short ferry ride from Islay, offers a more intimate whisky experience with its single distillery. The Jura Distillery produces a range of whiskies that are less peaty than their Islay counterparts, with a focus on rich, fruity flavors. The distillery tour provides a detailed look at Jura's unique production methods and concludes with a tasting in their cozy lounge, where you can savor the island's distinctive spirit while enjoying views of the Jura Mountains.

The Orkney Islands, located to the north of mainland Scotland, are home to two renowned distilleries: Highland Park and Scapa. Highland Park, with its Viking heritage, produces whiskies that are revered for their balance of sweetness and smoke. The distillery tour offers a deep dive into the unique factors that contribute to Highland Park's flavor, including the use of peat from Hobbister Moor and sherry-seasoned oak casks. Guests are treated to a tasting of Highland Park's core range, which showcases the complexity and harmony of their whiskies.

Scapa Distillery, often overshadowed by its neighbor, offers a different perspective on Orkney whisky, with a focus on unpeated, smooth, and honeyed expressions. The tour at Scapa is a more intimate affair, providing an opportunity to learn about their production techniques and enjoy a tasting of their signature expressions in the serene setting of the distillery's tasting room.

Beyond the individual distilleries, the Isles offer a wealth of whisky-related experiences that enhance any visit. Whisky festivals, such as the Islay Festival of Music and Malt (Fèis Ìle), provide a vibrant celebration of whisky culture, with tastings, masterclasses, and entertainment that attract whisky enthusiasts from around the world. These festivals offer an opportunity to engage with the local community, learn from industry experts, and experience the joy and camaraderie that whisky brings.

For those seeking a more personalized experience, private whisky tours offer tailored itineraries that cater to your specific interests and preferences. These tours often include visits to lesser-known distilleries, behind-the-scenes access, and exclusive tastings that provide a deeper understanding of the whisky-making process. Knowledgeable guides share stories and insights that enrich your appreciation of the craft, making for a truly memorable journey through the world of Scottish whisky.

As you travel through the Isles, it's important to consider the impact of whisky tourism and the role it plays in supporting local communities. Many distilleries are integral to the economies of their respective islands, providing employment and contributing to the preservation of traditional skills and practices. Choosing to support local businesses, whether through purchasing whisky, dining at local establishments, or staying in locally-owned accommodations, helps to ensure the continued vitality of these communities.

In conclusion, exploring the distilleries and whisky tours of the Scottish Isles offers more than just an opportunity to taste some of the world's finest whiskies. It provides a gateway into the history, culture, and landscapes that shape these unique spirits. Whether you're a seasoned whisky aficionado or a curious newcomer, the Isles offer a rich tapestry of experiences that will deepen your appreciation for Scotland's national drink. From the smoky depths of Islay to the gentle sweetness of Orkney, each sip tells a story, inviting you to savor the heart and soul of the Scottish Isles.

Coastal Walks and Marine Life

The rugged coastlines of the Scottish Isles are a tapestry of natural beauty, offering some of the most spectacular coastal walks and opportunities to observe diverse marine life. Each isle presents its own unique charm, with dramatic cliffs, secluded beaches, and a wealth of wildlife that thrives in these pristine environments. Whether you're an avid hiker or a casual wanderer, the coastal paths of the Isles invite you to explore their hidden wonders and connect with the natural world.

The Isle of Arran, often described as "Scotland in miniature," is a perfect starting point for those seeking diverse coastal walks. The island's varied terrain includes the Arran Coastal Way, a circular route that circumnavigates the island over 65 miles. This trail offers an ever-changing landscape, from the rugged cliffs of the north to the rolling farmland of the south. One highlight is the walk from Lochranza to Laggan, where the path hugs the coastline, providing stunning views across the Firth of Clyde and opportunities to spot seals basking on the rocks. As you traverse this route, the island's rich wildlife becomes apparent, with red deer often glimpsed in the hills and golden eagles soaring overhead.

Moving to the Outer Hebrides, the Isle of Harris offers a different kind of coastal experience. Known for its white sandy beaches and turquoise waters, Harris provides a serene setting for coastal exploration. The walk from Luskentyre to Seilebost is particularly enchanting, with a path that meanders along one of the most beautiful beaches in the UK. The shifting sands and crystal-clear sea create a tranquil atmosphere, perfect for observing the abundant birdlife, including oystercatchers and sandpipers. As the trail continues towards the Machair, a fertile strip of coastal grassland, you'll encounter a vibrant tapestry of wildflowers, home to an array of insects and small mammals.

The Isle of Mull, with its varied coastline, is another gem for those seeking coastal adventures. The walk from Calgary Bay to Treshnish Point is a highlight, offering dramatic views of the surrounding islands and the chance to spot marine life such as dolphins and porpoises. The path winds through a landscape of heather-clad hills and rocky outcrops, with the sound of the sea providing a constant accompaniment. As you approach Treshnish Point, the cliffs become a haven for seabirds, including puffins, guillemots, and razorbills, creating a cacophony of sound and activity.

For a more remote experience, the Isle of Jura offers a rugged and untamed coastline that promises solitude and a sense of adventure. The walk along the island's western coast, from Craighouse to the Corryvreckan Whirlpool, is a journey into the wild. This path, less trodden by visitors, offers stunning vistas of the Paps of Jura and the chance to encounter red deer, otters, and seals. The Corryvreckan Whirlpool, one of the largest tidal whirlpools in the world, is a sight to behold, with its powerful currents and swirling waters creating a dramatic natural spectacle.

The Orkney Islands, rich in history and natural beauty, also boast some of the most captivating coastal walks. The path from Yesnaby to Stromness offers a dramatic journey along towering sea cliffs, where the Atlantic waves crash against the rocks below. This walk is renowned for its geological features, including the Yesnaby Castle sea stack, and provides an opportunity to spot rare plants such as the Scottish primrose. The surrounding waters are home to a variety of marine life, and it's not uncommon to see seals and porpoises frolicking in the surf.

In addition to the scenic beauty and wildlife, the coastal walks of the Scottish Isles offer a chance to connect with the marine environment in a deeper way. Many of the Isles are involved in marine conservation efforts, with initiatives focused on protecting the rich biodiversity of the region. Visitors can participate in guided walks and activities that highlight the importance of preserving these fragile ecosystems. Local organizations often conduct beach clean-ups and citizen science projects, providing an opportunity to contribute to the conservation of these stunning coastlines.

The marine life of the Scottish Isles is as varied as the landscapes, with each isle offering unique opportunities to observe and learn about the creatures that inhabit these waters. The seas surrounding the Isles are home to a rich array of species, from the majestic minke whale to the playful common dolphin. The islands' rocky shores and kelp forests provide a habitat for a myriad of marine organisms, including crabs, starfish, and sea anemones. Snorkeling and diving excursions offer a closer look at this underwater world, revealing the vibrant colors and intricate ecosystems that lie beneath the waves.

For those interested in marine biology and conservation, the Scottish Isles offer numerous opportunities to engage with local experts and researchers. Many of the Isles have marine centers and research facilities that provide educational programs and workshops on marine ecology and conservation. These programs offer insights into the challenges facing marine environments and the efforts being made to protect them, fostering a greater appreciation for the delicate balance of life in the seas.

The coastal walks and marine life of the Scottish Isles provide a rich and rewarding experience, inviting visitors to explore and connect with the natural world in a meaningful way.

Whether you're traversing the rugged cliffs of Orkney, strolling along the sandy beaches of Harris, or witnessing the power of the Corryvreckan Whirlpool, each journey offers a unique perspective on the beauty and diversity of these remarkable islands. The Isles' commitment to conservation and sustainability ensures that these landscapes and ecosystems will continue to thrive, offering future generations the opportunity to experience their wonders. As you walk these coastal paths and encounter the marine life that calls the Isles home, you'll discover a deeper connection to the natural world and a profound appreciation for the enduring beauty of the Scottish Isles.

Local Culture and Island Life

Island life in the Scottish Isles offers a unique tapestry of cultural richness, shaped by centuries of history, tradition, and the distinct geographical isolation of each island. The communities here are resilient, their lifestyles molded by the rhythm of the sea and the changing seasons. As you step onto these islands, you enter a world where the past and present coexist in harmony, where local culture is not just a way of life but a reflection of the islands' identity.

The heartbeat of island life is the warm hospitality of its people. Islanders are known for their friendliness and welcoming nature, often eager to share stories and traditions with visitors. Social events like ceilidhs, community gatherings filled with music and dance, provide an excellent opportunity to immerse oneself in local culture. These events are a celebration of community spirit, where everyone, from the youngest to the oldest, participates in lively dances and traditional music played on fiddles and accordions. It's not uncommon for visitors to be invited to join in, experiencing firsthand the joy and camaraderie that these gatherings bring.

The Scottish Isles are steeped in Gaelic heritage, a cultural fabric that remains vibrant through language, music, and storytelling. On islands like the Outer Hebrides, Gaelic is still spoken daily, a testament to the resilience of this ancient language. Local schools teach Gaelic, ensuring that the younger generations remain connected to their roots. Visitors can experience this living tradition through Gaelic festivals and concerts, where traditional songs and poetry are performed, offering insights into the islanders' connection to their land and history.

Art and craftsmanship are integral to the cultural landscape of the Isles. Inspired by their rugged surroundings, island artists and artisans create works that reflect the beauty and spirit of their environment. From the intricate Harris Tweed, handwoven on the Isle of Harris, to pottery and jewelry crafted using local materials, the Isles offer a wealth of artistic expression. Many islands have galleries and craft shops where visitors can admire and purchase these unique creations, supporting local artisans and bringing a piece of the Isles' heritage into their own homes.

The islands' cuisine is another expression of local culture, deeply rooted in the land and sea that sustain them. Fresh seafood, including scallops, lobster, and salmon, features prominently on menus, while traditional dishes like cullen skink, a creamy fish soup, and bannocks, a type of flatbread, offer a taste of island life. Local produce, such as Orkney cheese and Shetland lamb, highlights the quality and flavor of the islands' agricultural bounty. Dining in the Isles is often a communal affair, with meals shared at local pubs and eateries where stories and laughter flow as freely as the whisky.

Island life is intrinsically linked to the natural world, and many islanders maintain a close relationship with the land and sea. Traditional practices such as crofting, a form of small-scale farming, continue to play a significant role in island communities. Crofters work the land, tending to sheep and cattle, growing crops, and living in harmony with the rhythms of nature. The crofting lifestyle embodies a deep respect for the land, passed down through generations, and remains vital to the islands' cultural and economic fabric.

The sea, too, is an ever-present influence, shaping the livelihoods and traditions of island communities. Fishing remains a cornerstone of island life, with many families involved in the industry for generations. The sight of fishing boats returning to harbor, laden with the day's catch, is a familiar and comforting one, a reminder of the islands' connection to the ocean. The sea is not just a source of sustenance but also a source of stories and legends, woven into the cultural narrative of the Isles.

Festivals and community events punctuate the island calendar, offering a glimpse into the vibrant cultural life of the Isles. Events such as the Hebridean Celtic Festival and the Orkney Folk Festival celebrate the rich musical heritage of the islands, attracting performers and audiences from near and far. These festivals are a showcase of talent and creativity, featuring a mix of traditional and contemporary music, workshops, and performances that highlight the diverse cultural influences at play.

Island life also embraces a slower pace, where the hustle and bustle of the mainland feels a world away. This unhurried

119

lifestyle offers a chance to disconnect from the demands of modern life and reconnect with nature and community. Islanders take pride in their close-knit communities, where everyone knows their neighbors, and the sense of belonging is strong. This slower pace allows for a deeper appreciation of the simple pleasures, from watching the sunset over the sea to sharing stories by the fire on a winter's night.

The challenges of island life, such as geographic isolation and harsh weather, have fostered a spirit of resilience and self-reliance among the islanders. These challenges have also encouraged innovation and adaptability, as communities find creative solutions to overcome the obstacles they face. This resourcefulness is evident in the many community projects and initiatives that promote sustainability and self-sufficiency, ensuring that island life remains vibrant for future generations.

In conclusion, the local culture and island life of the Scottish Isles offer a rich tapestry of experiences for those willing to immerse themselves in this unique world. From the warmth of its people to the beauty of its landscapes, the Isles provide a deep sense of connection to both the past and present. As you explore these islands, you'll discover a way of life that is deeply rooted in tradition yet open to change, a testament to the enduring spirit of the islanders and their unwavering love for their home. Whether it's through music, art, food, or simply the warmth of a shared smile, the Scottish Isles invite you to become part of their story, leaving a lasting impression that will stay with you long after you leave.

CHAPTER 5: CULINARY JOURNEY THROUGH SCOTLAND

Traditional Scottish Dishes

Traditional Scottish dishes are a reflection of the country's rich history, diverse landscapes, and the resourcefulness of its people. Scottish cuisine has evolved over centuries, influenced by the natural bounty of the land and the sea, as well as cultural exchanges with neighboring countries. The result is a tapestry of flavors and textures that tell the story of Scotland's past and present, offering a culinary journey that is both hearty and comforting.

One of the most iconic Scottish dishes is haggis, a savory pudding traditionally made from sheep's heart, liver, and lungs, mixed with onions, oatmeal, suet, and spices, all encased in the animal's stomach. Despite its humble ingredients, haggis is celebrated for its rich, earthy flavor and is a staple of Scottish cuisine. Often served with "neeps and tatties" (turnips and potatoes), haggis is a dish that embodies the frugality and ingenuity of Scottish cooking. It is famously celebrated on Burns Night, an annual event honoring Scotland's national poet, Robert Burns, who penned the famous "Address to a Haggis."

Another beloved dish is Cullen skink, a thick and creamy soup originating from the small town of Cullen in the northeast of Scotland. Made with smoked haddock, potatoes, and onions, Cullen skink is a comforting dish perfect for cold Scottish winters. The smokiness of the haddock, combined with the creamy texture of the potatoes, creates a deliciously warming meal that showcases the flavors of the sea.

Scotland's relationship with the sea is further highlighted in dishes like Arbroath smokies. These are haddock smoked over hardwood fires, a traditional method that imparts a distinctive flavor to the fish. The town of Arbroath, where this delicacy originated, is still home to many smokehouses where visitors can witness the process firsthand. Arbroath smokies are often served with bread and butter or used as an ingredient in fish pies and other seafood dishes.

Scotch broth is another classic Scottish dish, known for its hearty and nourishing qualities. This soup is made with lamb or mutton, barley, and an assortment of vegetables such as leeks, carrots, and turnips. Slow-cooked to perfection, Scotch broth is a testament to the Scottish preference for simple, wholesome meals that provide sustenance and warmth.

The Scots have a long tradition of baking, with many traditional breads and pastries that have been passed down through generations. Bannocks, a type of flatbread, are among the most well-known. Made from oats or barley, bannocks are baked on a griddle and can be either sweet or savory, depending on the ingredients used. They are often enjoyed with butter, cheese, or jam, making them a versatile staple in Scottish households.

Shortbread, with its crumbly texture and buttery flavor, is perhaps the most famous Scottish biscuit. Traditionally made with just three ingredients—flour, butter, and sugar— shortbread is a simple yet indulgent treat. It is often associated with special occasions and celebrations, such as Hogmanay, the Scottish New Year, where it is shared with family and friends.

Scotland's landscape provides a wealth of ingredients that are integral to its traditional dishes. Game meats such as venison, grouse, and pheasant are popular, particularly in the Highlands, where hunting has long been a way of life. Venison stew, slow-cooked with root vegetables and herbs, is a dish that highlights the rich, earthy flavors of the Scottish countryside.

The country's lush pastures and temperate climate are ideal for dairy farming, resulting in a variety of high-quality cheeses. Orkney cheddar, Isle of Mull cheese, and Lanark Blue are just a few examples of Scotland's diverse cheese offerings. These cheeses are often featured in traditional dishes or enjoyed on their own with oatcakes and a dram of whisky.

Speaking of whisky, this iconic Scottish spirit is not only enjoyed as a drink but also used as an ingredient in cooking. Whisky sauce, often served with haggis or steak, adds depth and complexity to a dish, while whisky-infused desserts like cranachan—a mix of whipped cream, honey, whisky, and raspberries layered with toasted oats—showcase the versatility of this beloved spirit.

Scottish cuisine is also influenced by its historical connections with other countries, leading to the incorporation of international flavors and techniques. For example, the Scottish love of curry is well-documented, with many Indian and Pakistani dishes adapted to suit local tastes. Chicken tikka masala, often cited as Britain's national dish, is believed to have been invented in Glasgow, illustrating the fusion of Scottish and South Asian culinary traditions.

In recent years, there has been a resurgence of interest in traditional Scottish dishes, with chefs and home cooks alike embracing the country's culinary heritage. This has led to a revival of old recipes and the creation of new ones that celebrate Scotland's rich food culture. Farmers' markets and food festivals across the country offer a chance to sample local produce and traditional dishes, while restaurants and gastropubs showcase the best of Scottish cuisine with a modern twist.

For those looking to experience traditional Scottish dishes at home, many recipes are readily available, allowing you to recreate the flavors of the Scottish Isles in your own kitchen. Ingredients such as oatmeal, smoked fish, and game meats can often be sourced from specialty stores or online retailers, ensuring that you have everything you need to embark on a Scottish culinary adventure.

Traditional Scottish dishes are a celebration of the country's history, culture, and natural resources. They offer a glimpse into the lives of the people who have called these islands home for centuries, revealing a deep connection to the land and sea. By exploring these dishes, you'll not only discover the rich flavors and textures of Scottish cuisine but also gain a deeper appreciation for the traditions and stories that have shaped this remarkable country. As you savor each bite, you'll be transported to the rugged landscapes and welcoming hearths of Scotland, where food is not just sustenance but a way of life.

Best Restaurants and Cafés

Navigating the culinary landscape of the Scottish Isles reveals a delightful array of restaurants and cafés that celebrate the rich flavors of the region. These establishments offer a fusion of traditional Scottish fare and innovative cuisine, each presenting a unique dining experience that reflects the local culture and the bounty of the land and sea. From cozy cafés nestled in picturesque villages to fine dining establishments with breathtaking views, the Isles are a haven for food lovers seeking to savor the essence of Scotland.

On the Isle of Skye, The Three Chimneys stands as a beacon of culinary excellence. Situated on the shores of Loch Dunvegan, this renowned restaurant has earned its reputation through a commitment to using the freshest local ingredients. The menu is a testament to the island's diverse offerings, with dishes that highlight the flavors of Skye's seafood, game, and produce. A meal here might begin with a starter of hand-dived scallops, followed by a main course of venison loin accompanied by foraged herbs and wild berries. The culinary journey is completed with a dessert that showcases Scotland's rich dairy heritage, such as a creamy buttermilk panna cotta.

Not far from The Three Chimneys, Skye's Loch Bay Restaurant offers an intimate dining experience with its focus on contemporary Scottish cuisine. Set in a charming whitewashed crofter's cottage, the restaurant specializes in seafood, with dishes that change with the seasons. The chef's tasting menu is a popular choice, allowing diners to sample an array of expertly crafted dishes that celebrate the freshest catches from the surrounding waters. Each plate is a work of art, combining bold flavors with delicate presentation.

On the Isle of Mull, Café Fish in Tobermory is a must-visit for seafood enthusiasts. Perched on the edge of the harbor, the café offers stunning views and a menu brimming with the day's freshest catch. The relaxed atmosphere makes it an ideal spot for enjoying a hearty bowl of seafood chowder or a platter of freshly shucked oysters. Café Fish's commitment to sustainability is evident in their sourcing practices, ensuring that each dish is not only delicious but also environmentally conscious.

For those exploring the Outer Hebrides, The Anchorage in Leverburgh is a hidden gem that combines traditional Scottish dishes with modern flair. Known for its welcoming atmosphere and attentive service, The Anchorage provides a taste of island hospitality at its finest. Diners can enjoy dishes like slow-cooked lamb shank with whisky sauce or a delicate seafood risotto, all crafted from locally sourced ingredients. The restaurant's location offers stunning views of the Harris coastline, making it a perfect spot to unwind after a day of exploration.

The Orkney Islands offer their own culinary delights, with Foveran Restaurant providing a memorable dining experience. Located on the outskirts of Kirkwall, Foveran features panoramic views of Scapa Flow and a menu that emphasizes the flavors of Orkney's seasonal produce. This family-run establishment prides itself on its use of locally sourced ingredients, with dishes like Orkney beef fillet and scallop ceviche showcasing the region's culinary heritage. Each meal is accompanied by a carefully curated selection of wines and whiskies, enhancing the overall experience.

In Lerwick, on the Shetland Islands, Fjara Café Bar offers a unique blend of café culture and contemporary dining. With its modern décor and relaxed atmosphere, Fjara is a popular spot for locals and visitors alike. The menu features a range of options, from hearty breakfasts and light lunches to indulgent dinners. Highlights include Shetland mussels in white wine sauce and homemade burgers crafted from Shetland-reared beef. Fjara's coffee and cake selection is equally impressive, making it a perfect stop for an afternoon treat while enjoying views of Lerwick harbor.

For a more traditional café experience, the Blue Lobster Café in Stornoway, Isle of Lewis, is a charming spot that offers a taste of authentic Hebridean hospitality. Known for its homemade baked goods and artisanal coffees, the Blue Lobster is a favorite among locals. Visitors can enjoy a slice of freshly baked cake or a warming bowl of cullen skink, a traditional Scottish soup, as they soak in the cozy atmosphere. The café also offers a selection of local crafts and souvenirs, providing an opportunity to take a piece of the Hebrides home with you.

In addition to these standout establishments, the Scottish Isles are home to numerous other eateries and cafés that offer their own unique take on island cuisine. Many of these places emphasize sustainability and local sourcing, reflecting the island communities' connection to their environment. Visitors are encouraged to explore beyond the well-known spots, as some of the most memorable dining experiences can be found in unexpected locations, where passionate chefs and welcoming hosts create meals that linger in the memory long after the plates are cleared.

The culinary scene of the Scottish Isles is a testament to the creativity and resilience of its people. Despite the challenges of geographic isolation and a harsh climate, these establishments thrive by focusing on the quality and authenticity of their offerings. The result is a vibrant tapestry of flavors that capture the essence of island life, inviting visitors to savor the taste of Scotland with each meal.

As you journey through the Isles, make time to explore the diverse range of restaurants and cafés that dot the landscape. Whether you're enjoying a leisurely lunch by the sea, indulging in a gourmet dinner, or simply sipping a cup of coffee in a cozy café, each experience offers a glimpse into the rich culinary heritage of the Scottish Isles. Embrace the opportunity to discover new flavors, meet passionate chefs, and immerse yourself in the warmth and hospitality that define the islands' dining culture. In doing so, you'll find that the taste of the Isles is as unforgettable as the landscapes themselves, leaving you with cherished memories of your culinary adventures in this remarkable corner of the world.

Farmers' Markets and Local Produce

Scotland's farmers' markets are vibrant showcases of the country's rich agricultural heritage, offering a delightful array of local produce that reflects the diverse landscapes and climates across the region. From the fertile plains of the Lowlands to the rugged hills of the Highlands, these markets provide a direct connection between consumers and the hardworking farmers and artisans who bring their goods to market. For both locals and visitors, exploring these markets offers a unique opportunity to experience Scotland's culinary wealth firsthand.

In the heart of Edinburgh, the farmers' market held at Castle Terrace is a bustling hub of activity every Saturday. With the iconic Edinburgh Castle as its backdrop, the market offers an impressive selection of fresh produce, artisanal cheeses, smoked fish, and handcrafted goods. Vendors proudly display their wares, often offering samples and engaging in friendly conversations with customers. A visit to this market is not just about shopping; it's an experience that immerses you in the community spirit and the passion of those who dedicate their lives to producing quality food.

Traveling to Glasgow, the city's vibrant farmers' markets reflect the diverse culinary influences that have shaped its food scene. The Partick Farmers' Market, held monthly, is a must-visit for those seeking locally sourced meats, organic vegetables, and freshly baked bread. The market is also a platform for emerging food entrepreneurs, showcasing innovative products like artisanal chocolates and gourmet sauces. This blend of traditional and modern offerings highlights Scotland's evolving food culture, where innovation meets heritage.

In the picturesque town of St. Andrews, the monthly farmers' market brings together producers from across Fife, a region renowned for its fertile land and high-quality produce. Here, you can find everything from freshly picked berries and seasonal vegetables to award-winning cheeses and homemade preserves. Strolling through the market, you'll likely encounter the Farmers' Market Food Trail, where local chefs demonstrate how to prepare dishes using the market's ingredients, offering inspiration for those looking to recreate the flavors of Scotland at home.

The Highlands offer their own unique farmers' market experiences, with Inverness Farmers' Market standing out as a highlight. Held on the first Saturday of each month, this market showcases the best of Highland produce, including venison, smoked salmon, and locally brewed ales. The market's location, in the heart of the city, provides a stunning backdrop of the River Ness, creating a picturesque setting for exploring the region's culinary offerings. As you wander through the stalls, the distinct flavors and aromas of the

Highlands come alive, revealing the deep connection between the land and its people.

Aberdeen, known as the "Granite City," is home to a thriving farmers' market scene, with the Belmont Street Farmers' Market offering a diverse selection of goods. From freshly baked scones and handmade chocolates to organic meats and dairy products, the market provides a taste of the North East's abundant produce. The market also emphasizes sustainability, with many vendors offering eco-friendly packaging and promoting zero waste initiatives. This commitment to environmental stewardship is a testament to the region's dedication to preserving its natural resources for future generations.

The Isle of Arran, often referred to as "Scotland in miniature," boasts its own farmers' market, where visitors can sample the island's renowned cheeses, organic vegetables, and freshly baked goods. The market is a celebration of the island's diverse produce, with vendors proudly showcasing their handmade chocolates, craft beers, and artisanal bread. Arran's farmers' market is not just a place to shop; it's a gathering point for the island community, where locals and visitors alike come together to share stories, recipes, and a love for quality food.

Beyond the larger cities and towns, farmers' markets can be found in many smaller communities across Scotland, each offering its own unique selection of local produce. In these markets, the emphasis is on quality and sustainability, with many vendors practicing organic farming and traditional methods of production. This commitment to preserving the integrity of their products ensures that consumers can enjoy food that is both delicious and environmentally responsible.

Exploring Scotland's farmers' markets provides a window into the country's rich culinary heritage and the dedication of those who work tirelessly to bring fresh, high-quality produce to market. These markets offer more than just a shopping experience; they are a celebration of community, tradition, and innovation. Whether you're sampling a freshly baked scone, savoring a slice of artisanal cheese, or chatting with a local farmer about their produce, each encounter is an opportunity to connect with the land and the people who nurture it.

In addition to the delicious foods available, Scotland's farmers' markets often feature live music, cooking demonstrations, and workshops, creating a lively and engaging atmosphere for visitors of all ages. These events provide an opportunity to learn more about Scotland's food culture and the techniques used to produce its renowned goods. From understanding the art of cheese-making to discovering the secrets of organic farming, these activities offer insights into the passion and skill that go into every product.

For those looking to explore Scotland's farmers' markets, planning a visit is easy, with most markets operating on weekends or monthly schedules. Many markets have websites or social media pages where you can find information about upcoming events, featured vendors, and special activities. This accessibility ensures that everyone, from locals to tourists, can experience the vibrant food culture that Scotland has to offer.

Scotland's farmers' markets are more than just places to buy food; they are gateways to the heart and soul of the country. Through these markets, you'll discover the stories behind the produce, the people who cultivate it, and the rich traditions that have shaped Scotland's culinary landscape. As you explore the stalls, sample the flavors, and engage with the community, you'll gain a deeper appreciation for the land and the bounty it provides. Whether you're a seasoned foodie or a curious traveler, the farmers' markets of Scotland promise a memorable and enriching experience that will leave you with a newfound love for the country's food and its people.

Whisky Tasting and Distilleries

Whisky, often referred to as the "water of life," is an intrinsic part of Scotland's cultural and historical identity. The art of whisky making has been perfected over centuries, and the country boasts a vast array of distilleries, each offering its own unique character and flavor profiles. For those embarking on a journey through Scotland, whisky tasting and distillery visits are essential experiences, providing a deeper understanding of the craftsmanship and passion that go into every bottle.

Scotland's whisky regions are renowned for producing distinct styles, each influenced by the local climate, landscape, and traditional methods. The country is divided into five main whisky-producing regions: Speyside, Islay, Highlands, Lowlands, and Campbeltown. Each region offers its own unique characteristics, allowing whisky enthusiasts to explore a diverse range of flavors and aromas that capture the essence of Scotland's natural beauty.

Speyside, located in the northeast of Scotland, is home to the highest concentration of distilleries in the country. Known for its smooth and complex whiskies, Speyside is characterized by flavors of honey, vanilla, and orchard fruits. Distilleries such as Glenfiddich and Macallan are legendary, offering tours and tastings that reveal the intricate process of whisky production.

Visitors can explore the lush landscapes along the River Spey, where the water sources are as integral to the whisky's character as the distilling process itself.

Islay, an island off the west coast of Scotland, is renowned for its bold and smoky whiskies. The peat bogs of Islay impart a distinctive smoky flavor to the whisky, creating a sensory experience that is both intense and memorable. Distilleries like Laphroaig, Ardbeg, and Lagavulin are celebrated for their peaty whiskies, each offering tours that delve into the unique peat-drying process and the island's maritime influence. The rugged beauty of Islay, with its windswept landscapes and dramatic coastline, provides a stunning backdrop for whisky exploration.

The Highlands, encompassing a vast area of Scotland, produce a diverse range of whisky styles. From the light and floral notes of Glenmorangie to the rich and robust flavors of Dalmore, Highland whiskies are as varied as the region's landscapes. Distillery visits in the Highlands often include breathtaking scenery, with many located near historic castles or nestled amidst rolling hills. The Highland whisky trail is a journey through both whisky heritage and the natural splendor of Scotland.

In the Lowlands, whiskies are typically lighter and more delicate, with flavors of citrus, grass, and floral notes. Distilleries such as Auchentoshan and Glenkinchie offer insights into the Lowland style, emphasizing triple distillation techniques that result in a smooth and refined spirit. The proximity of Lowland distilleries to major cities like Edinburgh and Glasgow makes them easily accessible for those seeking a taste of Scotland's whisky tradition without venturing too far from urban centers.

Campbeltown, once known as the "whisky capital of the world," is a small region with a rich whisky heritage. Today, only a handful of distilleries remain, including Springbank and Glen Scotia, but the quality and distinctiveness of Campbeltown whiskies are undeniable. Known for their complex flavors, with hints of maritime influence, these whiskies are cherished by connoisseurs. A visit to Campbeltown offers a glimpse into the history of whisky production and the enduring legacy of this storied town.

Whisky tasting is an art that engages the senses, requiring patience and attention to detail. When embarking on a tasting journey, it's essential to approach each whisky with an open mind, allowing the aromas and flavors to reveal themselves gradually. Begin by examining the color, which can offer clues about the whisky's age and maturation process. Swirling the glass gently releases the aromas, which should be inhaled deeply to capture the full spectrum of scents.

As you take a sip, let the whisky roll across your palate, noting the initial flavors and how they evolve over time. Consider the texture and mouthfeel, whether it's light and silky or rich and full-bodied. The finish, or aftertaste, is equally important, providing lasting impressions that linger long after the whisky is swallowed. Each whisky tells its own story, shaped by the choices of the distiller and the environment in which it was crafted.

Many distilleries offer guided tastings, led by knowledgeable experts who can provide insights into the nuances of each whisky. These experiences often include limited edition or cask-strength expressions, offering a rare opportunity to taste whiskies that are not widely available. Distillery tours also provide an in-depth look at the production process, from the malting of barley to the aging of whisky in oak casks. Witnessing the craftsmanship and dedication that goes into each bottle enhances the appreciation of Scotland's national drink.

For those looking to deepen their understanding of whisky, Scotland's whisky festivals are not to be missed. Events such as the Spirit of Speyside Whisky Festival and the Islay Festival of Music and Malt offer a celebration of whisky culture, with tastings, masterclasses, and distillery open days. These festivals provide a chance to meet fellow enthusiasts, learn from industry experts, and discover new favorites in a convivial and festive atmosphere.

When planning a whisky tasting tour, it's essential to consider logistics and accommodations. Many distilleries are located in remote areas, so arranging transportation and booking accommodations in advance is advisable. Some distilleries offer on-site lodgings or partner with local hotels to provide convenient options for visitors. Additionally, many tour operators offer guided whisky tours, allowing you to relax and enjoy the experience without the need for a designated driver.

Whisky tasting in Scotland is more than just a sensory experience; it's a journey into the heart of the country, exploring its landscapes, traditions, and the passion of its people. Each distillery visit and every dram of whisky offers a deeper connection to Scotland's rich history and cultural heritage. Whether you're a seasoned whisky aficionado or a curious newcomer, the experience of whisky tasting in

Scotland is an unforgettable adventure that invites you to savor the spirit of this remarkable land.

Cooking Classes and Food Tours

Cooking classes and food tours in Scotland offer a unique opportunity to delve deep into the country's rich culinary traditions and vibrant food culture. These experiences provide not only the chance to taste authentic Scottish dishes but also to learn the skills and techniques needed to recreate them at home. From bustling cities to serene countryside settings, Scotland's cooking classes and food tours cater to all levels of culinary expertise, from novices eager to learn the basics to seasoned cooks looking to expand their repertoire.

In the heart of Edinburgh, the Edinburgh New Town Cookery School is renowned for its comprehensive range of classes. Whether you're interested in mastering the art of baking traditional Scottish shortbread or crafting the perfect haggis, the school's expert instructors guide you through each step with patience and clarity. The school offers both day classes and longer courses, allowing participants to choose the format that best suits their schedule and interests. As you prepare dishes using locally sourced ingredients, you gain insights into the history and significance of each recipe, connecting with Scotland's culinary heritage on a deeper level.

For those seeking a more immersive experience, the Highlands provide a picturesque backdrop for cooking retreats that blend hands-on learning with the tranquility of nature. At the Ballintaggart Farm in Perthshire, participants can enjoy a farm-to-table experience that emphasizes sustainable and seasonal cooking. The farm's cooking classes focus on using ingredients grown on-site or sourced from nearby producers, allowing you to experience the full cycle of food production. As you cook, the instructors share stories of the land and the people who cultivate it, enriching your understanding of Scotland's agricultural traditions.

Food tours offer a different perspective on Scotland's culinary landscape, allowing participants to explore local markets, specialty shops, and hidden gems. In Glasgow, the Tasting Scotland tour takes you on a gastronomic journey through the city's diverse neighborhoods. From artisanal cheese shops to contemporary seafood restaurants, the tour showcases Glasgow's eclectic food scene. As you wander through the bustling streets, your guide shares anecdotes about the city's culinary evolution, highlighting the influence of various cultures and traditions on its cuisine.

The Isle of Skye, with its dramatic landscapes and rich culinary offerings, is a prime destination for food tours that combine breathtaking scenery with unforgettable meals. The Skye Food and Drink Trail guides visitors through the island's top food and drink producers, from whisky distilleries to artisanal bakeries. As you travel along the trail, you'll have the opportunity to sample local delicacies like smoked salmon, venison, and handmade chocolates, all while learning about the island's unique food culture and the people who bring these flavors to life.

In addition to organized tours and classes, Scotland's numerous food festivals provide a platform for culinary exploration and discovery. Events such as the Edinburgh Food Festival and the Taste of Shetland Festival celebrate the country's diverse food heritage, offering workshops, demonstrations, and tastings that cater to food enthusiasts of all ages. These festivals bring together chefs, producers, and food lovers, creating a vibrant atmosphere where you can engage with Scotland's culinary community and expand your culinary horizons.

For those looking to create a personalized culinary itinerary, many regions in Scotland offer bespoke cooking classes and tours that cater to individual preferences and interests. Whether you're passionate about seafood, game, or vegetarian cuisine, local chefs and guides can tailor experiences that highlight your chosen focus. These customized experiences offer an intimate and personalized approach to learning, allowing you to delve deeper into specific aspects of Scottish cuisine that captivate your interest.

To make the most of your cooking class or food tour, it's essential to approach each experience with an open mind and a willingness to learn. Engage with your instructors and guides, asking questions and seeking their insights into the dishes and ingredients you encounter. This interaction not only enhances your learning experience but also fosters a deeper appreciation for the skills and traditions that define Scottish cuisine.

When participating in cooking classes, take note of the techniques and tips shared by the instructors, as these can be invaluable when recreating the dishes at home. Pay attention to the balance of flavors, the importance of fresh ingredients, and the cultural significance of each recipe. By understanding the context and history behind the dishes, you'll be better equipped to infuse your own cooking with the essence of Scotland.

For those embarking on food tours, embrace the opportunity to taste a wide range of flavors and textures. Be adventurous in your choices, sampling dishes and ingredients you may not have encountered before. This willingness to explore new tastes will broaden your culinary palate and introduce you to the diverse world of Scottish food.

Document your experiences through notes and photographs, capturing the moments that resonate with you. These memories will serve as inspiration when you return to your own kitchen, allowing you to recreate the dishes and flavors that left a lasting impression. Share your newfound knowledge with friends and family, inviting them to join you on a culinary journey that celebrates the rich tapestry of Scottish cuisine.

Cooking classes and food tours in Scotland offer more than just a taste of local flavors; they provide a window into the country's soul, revealing the stories, traditions, and people who have shaped its culinary landscape. By participating in these experiences, you not only enhance your culinary skills but also forge a deeper connection with Scotland's rich cultural heritage. Whether you're a seasoned cook or a curious traveler, the journey of culinary discovery in Scotland is one that promises to enrich your understanding of food and leave you with cherished memories that last a lifetime.

CHAPTER 6: SCOTLAND'S RICH HISTORY AND LEGENDS

Ancient Sites and Monuments

Scotland's ancient sites and monuments are a testament to a land steeped in history and legend, where each stone whispers tales of a bygone era. From mysterious stone circles to imposing castles, these landmarks offer a glimpse into the lives, beliefs, and struggles of the people who have inhabited this storied land for millennia. For those eager to explore Scotland's rich historical tapestry, visiting these sites is an unforgettable journey through time.

The standing stones of Callanish, located on the Isle of Lewis, are among Scotland's most enigmatic ancient monuments. Erected around 5,000 years ago, these stones form a complex arrangement that has puzzled historians and archaeologists for generations. Their purpose remains shrouded in mystery, though some theories suggest they were used for astronomical observations or religious ceremonies. As you wander among the towering stones, it's easy to imagine the ancient rituals and gatherings that may have taken place here, connecting the people of the past with the cosmos above.

Further south, the Orkney Islands are home to a treasure trove of Neolithic sites, each offering a unique insight into the lives of Scotland's earliest inhabitants. Maeshowe, a magnificent chambered cairn, stands as a testament to the engineering prowess of these ancient builders. Constructed around 2800 BC, this tomb is aligned with the winter solstice, allowing sunlight to illuminate its inner chamber during the darkest days of the year. The experience of standing inside Maeshowe, surrounded by its massive stone walls, evokes a sense of awe and reverence for the people who crafted such a remarkable structure.

Nearby, the settlement of Skara Brae provides a rare glimpse into daily life during the Neolithic period. This remarkably well-preserved village, uncovered by a storm in 1850, consists of interconnected stone houses, complete with furniture carved from stone. Wandering through the settlement, one can almost hear the echoes of its long-ago inhabitants, as they went about their daily routines. Skara Brae offers invaluable insights into the social structure, economy, and domestic life of Scotland's earliest communities.

Moving eastward, the imposing fortress of Dunnottar Castle perches atop a sheer cliff overlooking the North Sea. With a history dating back over a thousand years, the castle has witnessed countless battles, sieges, and political intrigues. The ruins of Dunnottar tell tales of its strategic importance during the Wars of Scottish Independence and its role in safeguarding the Scottish Crown Jewels from Cromwell's forces. Exploring the castle's crumbling walls and hidden chambers, visitors can imagine the lives of those who defended this formidable stronghold against all odds.

The enigmatic hillfort of Traprain Law, located in East Lothian, offers another fascinating glimpse into Scotland's ancient past. This site was once a thriving center of power for the Votadini tribe, who inhabited the area during the Iron Age. Excavations have revealed a wealth of artifacts, including a remarkable hoard of Roman silver, suggesting a complex relationship between the indigenous tribes and the Roman Empire. Standing atop Traprain Law, with panoramic views of the surrounding landscape, one can sense the strategic importance of this site and the stories of diplomacy, trade, and conflict that unfolded here.

Among Scotland's most iconic monuments are its castles, each with its own unique history and legends. Stirling Castle, perched atop a volcanic rock, has played a central role in Scotland's history for centuries. As the site of numerous battles and royal ceremonies, Stirling was a key stronghold during the Wars of Scottish Independence. Visitors can explore the castle's grand halls and chambers, where kings and queens once held court, and marvel at the artistry of the Stirling Heads, intricately carved wooden medallions that adorn the ceilings.

Edinburgh Castle, dominating the skyline of Scotland's capital city, is another must-visit site for history enthusiasts. With its origins dating back to the 12th century, the castle has served as a royal residence, military stronghold, and symbol of Scottish resilience. Highlights of a visit to Edinburgh Castle include the Honours of Scotland, the oldest crown jewels in the British Isles, and the Stone of Destiny, a symbol of Scottish kingship. The castle's strategic position atop Castle Rock offers breathtaking views of the city and surrounding countryside, providing a fitting backdrop for its storied past.

The mystical landscape of the Scottish Highlands is dotted with ancient cairns and burial mounds, each with its own tales to tell. The Clava Cairns, located near Inverness, are a group of Bronze Age burial cairns set amidst a tranquil grove of trees. These cairns, with their circular chambers and standing stones, are thought to have been constructed for ceremonial purposes, possibly related to ancestor worship. Visiting the Clava Cairns, with their peaceful atmosphere and enigmatic presence, invites reflection on the spiritual beliefs and practices of Scotland's ancient peoples.

Further north, the mysterious Broch of Gurness offers a glimpse into the lives of Iron Age communities in Orkney. This well-preserved broch, a type of drystone tower unique to Scotland, is surrounded by a network of dwellings and defensive structures. The broch's imposing walls and intricate design speak to the ingenuity and resourcefulness of its builders, while the artifacts discovered at the site provide insights into the daily lives of its inhabitants.

Scotland's ancient sites and monuments are more than just remnants of the past; they are living connections to the stories, myths, and legends that have shaped the nation's identity. Whether exploring the windswept shores of the Outer Hebrides or the rolling hills of the Borders, each site offers a unique window into the lives of those who came before, inviting us to ponder the mysteries and marvels of Scotland's rich history.

To truly appreciate these ancient sites, it's essential to approach them with a sense of curiosity and respect. As you walk among the stones and ruins, take the time to absorb the atmosphere and imagine the lives of the people who once inhabited these places. Consider the cultural and historical context of each site, and how it fits into the broader tapestry of Scotland's past.

Many sites offer guided tours or visitor centers with informative exhibits, providing valuable context and enriching your understanding of the history and significance of each location. Engaging with knowledgeable guides and reading interpretive materials can enhance your experience, allowing you to form a deeper connection with Scotland's ancient heritage.

Scotland's ancient sites and monuments are a testament to the resilience, creativity, and spirit of its people, offering a journey through time that is both enlightening and inspiring. As you explore these remarkable landmarks, you'll discover the stories that have shaped Scotland's identity and gain a greater appreciation for the enduring legacy of its rich and varied history.

Famous Battles and Historic Events

The tapestry of Scotland's history is woven with numerous battles and historic events that have shaped the nation and its people. These events are not mere footnotes in history; they are pivotal moments that defined Scotland's identity and legacy. From legendary clashes on the battlefield to significant political upheavals, each event tells a story of resilience, courage, and the indomitable spirit of the Scots.

The Battle of Bannockburn, fought in 1314, stands as one of Scotland's most significant military victories. Under the leadership of King Robert the Bruce, the Scottish forces faced off against the much larger English army led by King Edward II. The battle was fought near Stirling, and despite being heavily outnumbered, the Scots utilized their knowledge of the terrain and strategic acumen to their advantage. The victory at Bannockburn was a turning point in the First War of Scottish Independence, solidifying Robert the Bruce's position as King of Scots and ensuring Scotland's sovereignty for years to come. The legacy of Bannockburn resonates through the ages, symbolizing the Scots' determination to remain free from English rule.

Another pivotal conflict, the Battle of Culloden, took place in 1746 on the windswept moorlands near Inverness. This battle marked the end of the Jacobite rising, a series of rebellions aimed at restoring the Stuart monarchy to the British throne. Led by Charles Edward Stuart, known as "Bonnie Prince Charlie," the Jacobite forces were ultimately defeated by the British army under the command of the Duke of Cumberland.

The defeat at Culloden had far-reaching consequences for the Scottish Highlands, leading to the suppression of the clan system and the enforcement of laws aimed at eradicating traditional Highland culture. The haunting desolation of Culloden Moor serves as a poignant reminder of the battle's impact on Scotland's history and the enduring legacy of the Jacobite cause.

Beyond the battlefield, Scotland's history is also marked by significant political events that have shaped the nation's identity. The signing of the Declaration of Arbroath in 1320 is one such moment. This letter, sent by Scottish nobles to Pope John XXII, asserted Scotland's status as an independent kingdom and defended Robert the Bruce's right to rule. It is regarded as a foundational document in the history of Scottish independence, highlighting the unity and resolve of the Scottish nobility in the face of external threats. The Declaration of Arbroath remains a powerful symbol of Scotland's national identity and the enduring quest for self-determination.

The Union of the Crowns in 1603 was a defining event that altered Scotland's political landscape. When Queen Elizabeth I of England died without an heir, the Scottish King James VI ascended to the English throne, becoming James I of England.

This union of the two crowns marked the beginning of a new era, as Scotland and England were governed by the same monarch. While the crowns were united, the two nations remained separate entities with their own parliaments and laws. This arrangement laid the groundwork for future political developments, including the eventual formation of the United Kingdom of Great Britain in 1707.

The Act of Union in 1707 was a watershed moment in Scotland's history, as it marked the unification of the Scottish and English parliaments. The decision to unite the two parliaments was met with mixed reactions in Scotland, with some viewing it as a betrayal of Scottish sovereignty while others saw it as an opportunity for economic growth and stability. The Act of Union paved the way for Scotland's integration into the British political and economic sphere, but it also sparked debates about national identity and autonomy that continue to resonate in contemporary Scottish politics.

Throughout the centuries, Scotland has also been a crucible of social and cultural change. The Scottish Enlightenment, which took place in the 18th century, was a period of intellectual and scientific flourishing that had a profound impact on the nation and the world. Figures such as philosopher David Hume, economist Adam Smith, and geologist James Hutton made groundbreaking contributions to their respective fields, shaping modern thought and advancing human knowledge. The ideas and innovations that emerged from the Scottish Enlightenment continue to influence contemporary society, underscoring Scotland's role as a beacon of progress and enlightenment.

The Highland Clearances, occurring mainly in the 18th and 19th centuries, were a tragic chapter in Scotland's history that reshaped the Highlands and its people. Landowners, seeking to maximize profits, forcibly evicted tenant farmers and replaced them with sheep farming. This led to widespread displacement and emigration, as many Highlanders were forced to leave their ancestral lands and seek new opportunities abroad. The Clearances had a lasting impact on the Highland landscape and culture, contributing to the diaspora of Scots around the world and altering the social fabric of the region.

More recently, the devolution of power to the Scottish Parliament in 1999 marked a significant milestone in Scotland's modern political history. Following a referendum, the establishment of the Scottish Parliament in Edinburgh granted Scotland greater autonomy over domestic affairs, including education, health, and transportation. This move was seen as a response to growing calls for self-governance and an acknowledgment of Scotland's distinct national identity within the United Kingdom. The Scottish Parliament has played a crucial role in shaping contemporary Scottish society, reflecting the aspirations and priorities of the Scottish people.

As we reflect on these famous battles and historic events, it becomes clear that Scotland's history is a tapestry of triumphs and trials, resilience and reinvention. Each event has left an indelible mark on the nation's identity, shaping the character and values of its people. From the fierce determination of the warriors at Bannockburn to the intellectual achievements of the Enlightenment, Scotland's history is a testament to the enduring spirit of a nation that has never ceased to strive for freedom, justice, and progress.

Exploring the sites and stories of these historic events offers a deeper understanding of Scotland's rich heritage and the forces that have shaped its destiny. Whether walking the fields of Culloden, pondering the significance of the Declaration of Arbroath, or engaging with the vibrant debates in the Scottish Parliament, each encounter with Scotland's past enriches our appreciation of its present and future. Through the lens of history, we gain insight into the indomitable spirit of Scotland and the enduring legacy of its people.

Myths and Legends of Scotland

Scotland's myths and legends are woven into the very fabric of its landscape, echoing through misty glens, rugged highlands, and ancient lochs. These stories, passed down through generations, capture the imagination with tales of mystical creatures, heroic deeds, and otherworldly realms. They offer a glimpse into the cultural and spiritual life of a nation where the line between reality and myth is often beautifully blurred.

One of the most famous legends is that of the Loch Ness Monster, affectionately known as "Nessie." Nestled in the depths of Loch Ness, this elusive creature has captured the world's attention for decades. Sightings and accounts of Nessie date back to the 6th century, when the Irish monk Saint Columba reportedly encountered a "water beast" in the River Ness. Over the years, numerous sightings have been reported, sparking curiosity and debate. Whether viewed as a prehistoric creature, a spirit of the loch, or a figment of imagination, Nessie remains an enduring symbol of Scotland's mysterious allure.

The legend of the Kelpie adds another layer of enchantment to Scotland's waterways. These shape-shifting water spirits are said to inhabit rivers and lochs, often appearing as majestic horses. According to folklore, Kelpies can lure unsuspecting travelers onto their backs, dragging them to a watery grave. One of the most famous Kelpie tales is that of the Loch Garve Kelpie, which was said to have been captured and tamed by a cunning blacksmith. The Kelpie's story reflects the power and danger of Scotland's natural elements, serving as a cautionary tale about the untamed forces of nature.

In the realm of the Highlands, the legend of the Selkies enchants with tales of love and transformation. Selkies are mythical beings capable of shedding their seal skins to assume human form. According to lore, they often fall in love with humans, but their longing for the sea ultimately draws them back to the ocean. The stories of Selkies are imbued with themes of longing, loss, and the duality of existence. In some variations, a human discovers a Selkie's hidden skin, compelling the creature to remain on land until the skin is returned. These tales evoke the timeless struggle between freedom and attachment, resonating with those who hear them.

The tale of the legendary warrior and king, Robert the Bruce, is interwoven with mythic elements that highlight the virtues of perseverance and courage. According to legend, after suffering a series of defeats, Robert the Bruce found inspiration in the determination of a spider attempting to spin its web. Witnessing the spider's relentless efforts, Bruce resolved to persist in his own battles, ultimately leading to his victory at the Battle of Bannockburn. This tale, blending historical fact with legend, underscores the enduring spirit of resilience that characterizes Scotland's national identity.

Scotland's ancient landscape is also home to the mystical realm of the Fairy Folk, or "sìth" in Gaelic. These otherworldly beings are said to inhabit the hidden places of nature, including hilltops, forests, and stone circles. According to folklore, Fairy Folk are both benevolent and mischievous, capable of bestowing blessings or causing mischief. The tales of the Fairy Folk are rich with enchantment, describing their magical dances, music, and occasional interactions with humans. The Fairy Pools on the Isle of Skye, with their crystal-clear waters and ethereal beauty, are believed to be a gathering place for these mystical beings, drawing visitors seeking a glimpse of the otherworldly.

The story of MacBeth, immortalized by William Shakespeare, is steeped in legend and historical intrigue. The real MacBeth was a Scottish king who reigned in the 11th century, but his life diverges significantly from the tragic figure portrayed in Shakespeare's play. The play's supernatural elements, including the prophecy of the three witches and the ghostly apparitions, have contributed to the legend of MacBeth as a tale of ambition and fate. This fusion of history and myth has left an indelible mark on Scotland's cultural landscape, inviting exploration of the themes of power, destiny, and the supernatural.

The legend of the Blue Men of the Minch is a captivating maritime myth that speaks to the perils of the sea. These blue-skinned creatures are said to inhabit the waters between the mainland and the Isle of Lewis, challenging sailors who venture into their domain. According to legend, the Blue Men can conjure storms and wreck ships, unless their riddles are answered correctly. The tale of the Blue Men reflects the treacherous nature of Scotland's coastal waters, serving as a reminder of the respect and caution required when navigating them.

The myths and legends of Scotland are not merely tales of fantasy; they are a reflection of the collective consciousness of a people deeply connected to their land and history. These stories convey universal themes of love, bravery, and the eternal struggle between good and evil, resonating with audiences across time and place. They offer a window into the values, beliefs, and fears of generations past, while inviting contemporary audiences to explore the boundaries of imagination and reality.

Exploring these myths and legends is a journey into the heart of Scotland's cultural heritage, where each story is a thread in the intricate tapestry of the nation's identity. Whether it's the haunting allure of the lochs, the enchanting melodies of the Fairy Folk, or the heroic deeds of legendary figures, these tales invite us to delve into the mysteries of the past and discover the timeless truths they hold. By embracing the myths and legends of Scotland, we connect with a rich tradition of storytelling that continues to inspire wonder and curiosity in all who encounter it.

Museums and Heritage Centers

Scotland's museums and heritage centers serve as vibrant portals to the past, offering visitors an immersive experience into the country's rich tapestry of history and legend. These institutions are custodians of Scotland's cultural legacy, preserving artifacts, stories, and traditions that define the Scottish identity. From bustling cities to remote villages, each museum and heritage center provides a unique perspective on the nation's journey through time, inviting exploration and discovery.

The National Museum of Scotland in Edinburgh stands as a beacon of Scottish heritage, its impressive architecture housing a treasure trove of artifacts that span centuries. The museum's diverse collection offers insights into Scotland's natural history, archaeology, and cultural evolution. From the awe-inspiring Lewis Chessmen, intricately carved from walrus ivory, to the majestic skeleton of a Tyrannosaurus rex, the exhibits captivate the imagination and spark curiosity. The museum's interactive displays and engaging storytelling bring history to life, making it accessible to visitors of all ages.

In the heart of Glasgow, the Kelvingrove Art Gallery and Museum is a beloved institution that showcases Scotland's artistic and historical treasures. Housed in a stunning Spanish Baroque-style building, the museum's extensive collection includes works by renowned artists such as Salvador Dalí and Charles Rennie Mackintosh. The museum also delves into Scotland's social history, with exhibits that explore the country's industrial heritage, cultural diversity, and contributions to science and innovation. Kelvingrove's dynamic and diverse offerings ensure a captivating experience for anyone eager to explore the intersection of art and history.

Venturing into the Highlands, the Culloden Battlefield and Visitor Centre offers a poignant exploration of one of Scotland's most significant historical events. The center provides a comprehensive account of the 1746 Battle of Culloden, where the Jacobite forces suffered a devastating defeat. Through immersive exhibits, including a 360-degree battle immersion theater, visitors gain a deeper understanding of the battle's impact on Scotland's history and culture. The site's preservation and educational efforts honor the memory of those who fought and died on the moor, offering a solemn reflection on the past.

In Orkney, the Orkney Museum provides an intimate glimpse into the archipelago's rich history and archaeological significance. Located in the historic town of Kirkwall, the museum's exhibits trace the story of Orkney from the Stone Age to the present day. Artifacts from the Neolithic village of Skara Brae and the enigmatic Maeshowe chambered cairn offer a window into the lives of Orkney's ancient inhabitants. The museum also celebrates the islands' Norse heritage, highlighting the cultural influences that have shaped Orkney's unique identity.

The Highland Folk Museum in Newtonmore offers a fascinating journey into Scotland's rural past, with a focus on the everyday lives of Highland people. This open-air museum spans over eighty acres and features reconstructed buildings, from traditional blackhouses to a working 1930s croft. Visitors can experience hands-on demonstrations of traditional crafts and activities, such as weaving and peat cutting, gaining insight into the resilience and resourcefulness of Highland communities. The museum's immersive approach provides an engaging and educational experience, bringing Scotland's rural heritage to life.

In the town of Stirling, the Bannockburn Visitor Centre commemorates the pivotal 1314 Battle of Bannockburn, a defining moment in Scotland's quest for independence. The center's state-of-the-art 3D battle simulation offers a thrilling and educational experience, allowing visitors to relive the battle from both Scottish and English perspectives. Interactive exhibits delve into the strategies, weapons, and key figures of the conflict, providing a comprehensive understanding of the battle's significance. The visitor center's engaging approach ensures that the legacy of Bannockburn continues to inspire and educate future generations.

Scotland's maritime heritage is celebrated at the Scottish Maritime Museum, with locations in Irvine and Dumbarton. The museum's collections highlight the country's rich shipbuilding and seafaring history, showcasing a variety of vessels, from steam-powered tugboats to sleek racing yachts. The exhibits also explore the lives of the people who worked in the maritime industry, offering a glimpse into the challenges and triumphs of life at sea. The museum's dedication to preserving Scotland's maritime legacy ensures that the stories of its seafarers and shipbuilders are shared and remembered.

The Shetland Museum and Archives, located in Lerwick, offers a comprehensive exploration of the unique history and culture of the Shetland Islands. The museum's exhibits trace the islands' history from prehistoric times to the present day, highlighting the influences of Norse, Scottish, and maritime traditions. Artifacts such as intricately carved Pictish stones and traditional Shetland knitwear offer insights into the islands' rich heritage. The museum also celebrates Shetland's vibrant cultural scene, showcasing contemporary art, music, and storytelling that reflect the islands' enduring creativity and spirit.

In the picturesque town of St. Andrews, the British Golf Museum pays homage to Scotland's status as the birthplace of golf. The museum's collection chronicles the evolution of the sport, from its origins in the 15th century to its modern-day global influence. Exhibits feature historic clubs, balls, and memorabilia, as well as interactive displays that explore the science and artistry of the game. The museum's location near the renowned Old Course adds to its appeal, making it a must-visit destination for golf enthusiasts and history buffs alike.

The V&A Dundee, Scotland's first design museum, celebrates the country's contributions to the world of design and innovation. Located on the banks of the River Tay, the museum's striking architecture is a testament to Scotland's creative spirit. The museum's exhibits explore a wide range of design disciplines, from fashion and architecture to digital technology and engineering. Through its collections and programs, the V&A Dundee fosters a deeper appreciation for the role of design in shaping our world and inspires future generations of creators and innovators.

Scotland's museums and heritage centers are more than repositories of artifacts; they are dynamic spaces that engage, educate, and inspire. By preserving and interpreting the nation's history and culture, these institutions ensure that Scotland's rich heritage is accessible to all. Whether exploring the ancient mysteries of Orkney, the creative genius of Charles

Rennie Mackintosh, or the enduring legacy of Bannockburn, visitors are invited to embark on a journey of discovery that celebrates the spirit and resilience of the Scottish people.

These museums and heritage centers serve as bridges between the past and present, connecting us with the stories and traditions that have shaped Scotland's identity. Through their diverse and engaging offerings, they encourage us to reflect on our shared history and consider the enduring impact of the past on our lives today. As we explore these cultural treasures, we gain a deeper understanding of Scotland's rich heritage and the timeless narratives that continue to inspire and captivate.

Tracing Ancestry and Family History

Scotland's intricate tapestry of history and legend is mirrored in the personal stories of its people, each thread representing an individual life interwoven with the broader narrative of the nation. Tracing one's ancestry and family history in Scotland is a journey into this rich cultural mosaic, offering a sense of connection to the past and an understanding of the forces that shaped one's identity. For many, this journey begins with a curiosity about familial roots, leading to the discovery of stories that resonate through generations.

Embarking on this quest often starts with gathering information from family records and oral histories. Conversations with relatives can unearth valuable details about ancestors, including names, birthplaces, occupations, and significant life events. Family heirlooms, letters, and photographs serve as tangible links to the past, providing insights into the lives of those who came before. Documenting this information is crucial, as it forms the foundation upon which further research can be built.

Once a basic family tree is established, the next step involves delving into Scotland's extensive archival resources. The National Records of Scotland, located in Edinburgh, is a treasure trove of genealogical information. It houses a vast collection of census records, birth, marriage, and death certificates, wills, and legal documents dating back centuries. These records offer a detailed glimpse into the lives of Scots throughout history, illuminating their personal stories and societal roles.

The ScotlandsPeople website is an invaluable online resource that provides access to many of these records. With its user-friendly interface, individuals can search for and obtain digital copies of vital records, making it easier to piece together their family history from afar. The site offers various search options, enabling researchers to navigate through historical documents efficiently. Accessing these documents can provide a wealth of information, from verifying family legends to uncovering unknown ancestors.

For those with roots in the Highlands and Islands, the Highland Archives Network offers region-specific resources. This network comprises several archive centers scattered across the Highlands, each holding unique collections pertinent to their areas. These centers provide access to estate records, parish registers, and local histories, offering a comprehensive view of life in the Highlands over the centuries. Exploring these archives can reveal fascinating stories of resilience and adaptation, shedding light on the experiences of Highland ancestors.

Clan histories and genealogies are another rich source of information for those tracing Scottish ancestry. Clans have played a significant role in Scotland's social structure, and many families have strong ties to specific clans. Exploring clan histories can provide context for familial connections and offer a sense of belonging to a larger community. Many clans have dedicated societies and websites that offer resources for genealogical research, including clan-specific records and publications.

Local heritage centers and libraries throughout Scotland also offer valuable resources for genealogical research. These institutions often hold unique collections of historical documents, newspapers, and maps that are not available elsewhere. Local knowledge and expertise can be invaluable, as staff members can provide guidance and insights into regional history and genealogical research techniques. Visiting these centers can enrich the research process and offer new perspectives on family stories.

DNA testing has become an increasingly popular tool for tracing ancestry, providing insights into genetic heritage and connections to distant relatives. Several companies offer DNA testing services that can reveal ethnic origins and identify potential relatives through shared DNA. While DNA testing is a powerful tool, it is most effective when used in conjunction with traditional genealogical research. The combination of genetic data and historical records can help confirm family connections and unravel complex genealogical puzzles.

For those with ancestors who emigrated from Scotland, the Scottish Emigration Database is an essential resource. This database, managed by the University of Edinburgh, contains information on thousands of Scots who emigrated between

1890 and 1960. It provides details about their destinations, occupations, and family members, offering a glimpse into the reasons behind their journeys and the lives they built abroad. This resource is particularly valuable for those tracing family lines across continents, as it helps bridge the gap between Scottish and international records.

Engaging with genealogical societies and online forums can further enhance the research process. These communities offer opportunities to connect with fellow researchers, share tips, and exchange information. Collaborative research can lead to the discovery of new resources, insights, and connections, enriching the understanding of one's family history. Many societies offer workshops, webinars, and publications that provide guidance on research techniques and Scottish history, empowering individuals to delve deeper into their ancestral roots.

As the journey of tracing ancestry unfolds, it is essential to approach the process with patience and an open mind. Genealogical research is often a meticulous endeavor, requiring careful documentation and verification of information. It is not uncommon to encounter challenges, such as conflicting records or elusive ancestors. However, these obstacles are part of the journey, offering opportunities to develop problem-solving skills and creativity in research.

Exploring family history is not merely an exercise in uncovering names and dates; it is an opportunity to connect with the stories and experiences of those who came before. Each discovery adds depth to the narrative of one's ancestry, revealing the triumphs, struggles, and aspirations of ancestors who played a role in shaping the present. These stories offer a sense of belonging and continuity, linking past and present in a shared journey through time.

As the tapestry of family history is woven, the threads of individual lives come together to form a rich and vibrant picture of Scotland's heritage. Whether uncovering tales of Highland clans, maritime adventures, or urban settlers, each story contributes to the broader narrative of Scotland's past. Through the exploration of ancestry, individuals gain a deeper appreciation for the resilience and spirit of their forebears, as well as a profound connection to the land and culture that shaped them.

In the end, tracing ancestry and family history is a journey of discovery and reflection, inviting individuals to explore the intricate web of connections that define their identity. It is a journey that honors the past while enriching the present, offering insights into the enduring legacy of Scotland's history and legends. Through this exploration, the stories of ancestors come alive, resonating with timeless themes of love, courage, and the unbreakable bonds of family.

CHAPTER 7: OUTDOOR ADVENTURES AND ACTIVITIES

Hiking and Trekking Trails

Scotland's breathtaking landscapes offer a haven for outdoor enthusiasts, with hiking and trekking trails that wind through some of the most stunning scenery in the world. From the rugged Highlands to the serene lochs and coastline, the variety of trails provides both novice and experienced hikers the opportunity to immerse themselves in the natural beauty and rich history of the land.

The West Highland Way is one of Scotland's most iconic long-distance trails, stretching 96 miles from Milngavie, just outside Glasgow, to Fort William in the heart of the Highlands. This trail takes hikers through a diverse range of landscapes, beginning with gentle woodland paths and rolling hills before ascending into the dramatic expanse of Rannoch Moor. The journey culminates with the breathtaking views of Ben Nevis, the UK's highest peak. The trail is well-marked, with numerous accommodations and services along the route, making it accessible for hikers of varying skill levels. The West Highland Way encapsulates the spirit of Scottish adventure, offering a rewarding trek through some of the country's most iconic scenery.

For those seeking a more challenging experience, the Cape Wrath Trail presents a formidable yet rewarding journey. This unofficial and unmarked route stretches approximately 230 miles from Fort William to Cape Wrath, the northwesternmost point of mainland Britain. The trail traverses remote and rugged terrain, requiring excellent navigation skills and a high level of fitness. Hikers will encounter diverse landscapes, from the dramatic peaks of the Northwest Highlands to the wild and windswept coastline. The Cape Wrath Trail is often referred to as Britain's toughest long-distance walk, but for those who undertake it, the sense of solitude and connection with nature is unparalleled.

The Isle of Skye offers a variety of hiking opportunities, with trails that showcase the island's unique geological features and breathtaking vistas. The Quiraing, a landslip on the Trotternish Ridge, presents an otherworldly landscape of pinnacles, cliffs, and hidden plateaus. The circular route around the Quiraing is approximately 4.5 miles and offers hikers the chance to explore this dramatic terrain while enjoying panoramic views of the surrounding sea and islands. For a more challenging hike, the ascent of the Black Cuillin offers an exhilarating adventure. These jagged peaks are renowned for their technical difficulty and require experience in scrambling and mountaineering.

The Great Glen Way is another popular long-distance trail, stretching 79 miles from Fort William to Inverness. This trail follows the natural fault line of the Great Glen, passing through a series of lochs, including the famous Loch Ness. The route offers a mix of canal towpaths, forest tracks, and open moorland, providing a diverse hiking experience. The Great Glen Way is well-suited for those seeking a more leisurely trek, with ample opportunities to explore the cultural and historical sites along the way, such as Urquhart Castle on the shores of Loch Ness.

For a coastal hiking experience, the Fife Coastal Path offers a delightful journey along Scotland's east coast. This 117-mile trail stretches from Kincardine to Newburgh, passing through charming fishing villages, sandy beaches, and dramatic cliffs. Hikers can explore the rich history and wildlife of the region, with highlights including the picturesque town of St Andrews, renowned for its historic university and golf course. The Fife Coastal Path is well-marked and accessible, making it an excellent choice for hikers of all abilities seeking to experience Scotland's coastal charm.

The Southern Upland Way is Scotland's coast-to-coast route, spanning 214 miles from Portpatrick on the west coast to Cockburnspath on the east coast. This trail traverses the rolling hills and moorlands of the Southern Uplands, offering hikers a journey through some of Scotland's lesser-known landscapes. The trail is challenging, with varied terrain and remote sections, but rewards hikers with stunning views and a sense of accomplishment. The Southern Upland Way provides a unique perspective on Scotland's countryside, with opportunities to spot wildlife and explore historic sites along the route.

For those interested in exploring Scotland's national parks, the Cairngorms National Park offers a wealth of hiking opportunities. The park is home to five of the UK's six highest peaks, as well as ancient forests, rivers, and lochs. Hikers can choose from a variety of trails, ranging from gentle woodland walks to challenging mountain ascents. The ascent of Ben Macdui, Scotland's second-highest peak, offers a rewarding hike with panoramic views of the Cairngorm plateau. The park's diverse landscapes and abundant wildlife make it a must-visit destination for outdoor enthusiasts.

The Loch Lomond and The Trossachs National Park is another area rich in hiking opportunities. The park's diverse landscapes include rolling hills, tranquil lochs, and rugged mountains. The ascent of Ben Lomond, a popular Munro, offers hikers a relatively accessible mountain experience with stunning views of Loch Lomond and the surrounding area. For a more leisurely hike, the Three Lochs Way provides a scenic route through the heart of the park, passing by Loch Lomond, Loch Long, and Loch Gare.

When hiking in Scotland, it's essential to be prepared for the country's unpredictable weather. Even in summer, conditions can change rapidly, so it's crucial to carry appropriate clothing and gear. Waterproofs, sturdy footwear, and a map and compass are essential for safe navigation. Many trails pass through remote areas, so hikers should be self-sufficient and carry enough food and water for the journey.

With its diverse landscapes and rich history, Scotland offers a wealth of hiking and trekking experiences for outdoor enthusiasts. Whether traversing iconic long-distance trails or exploring the rugged beauty of the Highlands and islands, hikers are rewarded with breathtaking views and a deep connection to the land. Each trail tells a story, inviting hikers to step into the pages of Scotland's natural and cultural heritage.

Cycling Routes and Tours

Cycling through Scotland offers an unparalleled way to experience the country's breathtaking landscapes, vibrant culture, and rich history. With routes that cater to all levels of cyclists, from leisurely riders to seasoned athletes, Scotland's cycling trails provide an adventurous and immersive way to explore the nation's diverse regions. Whether pedaling along coastal paths, navigating through lush valleys, or tackling challenging mountain terrains, cyclists are afforded a unique perspective on Scotland's natural beauty and cultural heritage.

One of the most famous cycling routes in Scotland is the North Coast 500, often referred to as Scotland's answer to Route 66. This 516-mile loop begins and ends in Inverness, taking cyclists on an epic journey around the north coast of Scotland. The route offers a mix of stunning coastal scenery, rugged landscapes, and charming villages. Highlights include the dramatic cliffs of Cape Wrath, the pristine beaches of Durness, and the historic castles that dot the countryside. With numerous opportunities for wild camping and local hospitality, the North Coast 500 is a must for those seeking a cycling adventure that captures the essence of Scotland's wild beauty.

For cyclists looking to explore Scotland's islands, the Hebridean Way offers an unforgettable experience. Stretching 185 miles from Vatersay in the south to the Butt of Lewis in the north, this route traverses ten islands in the Outer Hebrides, connected by causeways and ferries. The Hebridean Way showcases the unique landscapes and cultures of the islands, from the white sandy beaches of Harris to the rugged hills of Lewis. Cyclists can enjoy the solitude of the remote islands, the warmth of the island communities, and the chance to spot wildlife such as seals, otters, and eagles. The Hebridean Way is a journey through landscapes shaped by wind and sea, offering a peaceful escape from the hustle and bustle of modern life.

For those who prefer a more leisurely pace, the Lochs and Glens Cycle Route offers a scenic journey through some of Scotland's most beautiful landscapes. This National Cycle Network route stretches from Glasgow to Inverness, passing through the Loch Lomond and The Trossachs National Park and the Cairngorms National Park. The route is primarily on quiet roads and dedicated cycle paths, making it suitable for families and less experienced cyclists. Along the way, cyclists can explore picturesque towns such as Callander and Pitlochry, visit historic sites like Urquhart Castle on Loch Ness, and enjoy the stunning scenery of lochs, forests, and mountains.

Mountain biking enthusiasts will find plenty of thrills in Scotland's dedicated trail centers. The 7stanes, a network of seven mountain biking centers located in the south of Scotland, offers world-class trails for riders of all abilities. Each center features a range of trails, from gentle green routes for beginners to challenging black and red trails for experienced riders. The Glentress Forest, part of the 7stanes, is one of the most popular destinations, with trails that provide exhilarating rides through forested hills and stunning views of the surrounding landscapes. The centers also offer facilities such as bike rentals, cafes, and showers, ensuring that riders have everything they need for a day of adventure on the trails.

The Isle of Arran, often referred to as "Scotland in Miniature," is a cyclist's paradise with its diverse landscapes and accessible terrain. The island's 55-mile circumference offers a manageable day ride, with opportunities to explore charming villages, ancient stone circles, and the stunning scenery of Goatfell, Arran's highest peak. The island's quiet roads and varied terrain make it an ideal destination for cyclists of all levels, while the local hospitality and culinary delights add to the experience. Arran's compact size allows cyclists to enjoy a comprehensive tour of its highlights in a short time, making it a perfect getaway for a cycling weekend.

For a truly unique cycling experience, the Caledonia Way offers a journey through Scotland's Great Glen. This 234-mile route stretches from Campbeltown on the Kintyre Peninsula to Inverness, following the natural fault line of the Great Glen. The route includes a mix of quiet roads, forest tracks, and canal towpaths, providing a varied and engaging ride. Cyclists will pass through the historic towns of Oban and Fort William, enjoy views of Ben Nevis, and cycle alongside the Caledonian Canal and Loch Ness. The Caledonia Way offers a blend of cultural and natural attractions, making it a rewarding journey for those seeking to explore the heart of Scotland.

When planning a cycling tour in Scotland, it's essential to consider the country's variable weather and prepare accordingly. Layers of clothing, waterproof gear, and a reliable map or GPS device are crucial for a safe and enjoyable ride. Scotland's cycling routes often pass through remote areas, so cyclists should be self-sufficient and carry enough food and water for their journey. Additionally, respecting the countryside and adhering to the Scottish Outdoor Access Code ensures that the natural beauty of the landscapes is preserved for future generations.

Cycling in Scotland is not just about the destination; it's about the journey and the experiences along the way. Each route offers its own unique blend of challenges and rewards, inviting cyclists to connect with the land, its history, and its people. Whether exploring the windswept coasts, the tranquil lochs, or the majestic mountains, cyclists are treated to a sense of freedom and adventure that is uniquely Scottish. The country's diverse cycling routes and tours provide endless opportunities for exploration and discovery, inviting riders to embark on an unforgettable journey through one of the world's most captivating landscapes.

Water Sports and Activities

Scotland's diverse waterways and rugged coastlines provide an exhilarating playground for water sports enthusiasts, offering a range of activities that cater to both adrenaline seekers and those looking for a more tranquil experience. From the wild waves of the Atlantic Ocean to the serene lochs nestled in the Highlands, Scotland's aquatic adventures promise unforgettable experiences against the backdrop of some of the world's most stunning natural scenery.

Surfing in Scotland may not be the first thing that comes to mind, but the country's northern coastlines offer some of Europe's best surfing conditions. Thurso, located on the north coast, is renowned for its powerful waves and has hosted numerous international surfing competitions. The cold waters and challenging conditions attract experienced surfers from around the world, eager to ride the renowned reef breaks that make Thurso a top surfing destination. For those new to the sport, several surf schools along the coast provide lessons and equipment rentals, allowing beginners to safely experience the thrill of catching their first wave.

Kayaking and canoeing are popular ways to explore Scotland's lochs and rivers, offering a peaceful and intimate connection with nature. The country boasts a wealth of paddling routes, from gentle flat-water lochs to challenging white-water rivers. Loch Lomond, the largest freshwater loch in Scotland, is a favorite destination for kayakers, with its calm waters and picturesque islands. Paddlers can explore the loch's many inlets and bays, enjoying the stunning views of the surrounding hills and forests. For a more adventurous experience, the River Tay offers exciting white-water sections, particularly around the town of Aberfeldy, where paddlers can test their skills against the river's rapids.

Scotland's coastline is dotted with numerous sea kayaking opportunities, providing access to remote beaches, sea caves, and abundant wildlife. The west coast, with its sheltered bays and dramatic cliffs, is particularly popular with sea kayakers. The Sound of Arisaig, for example, offers a stunning backdrop of the Small Isles and the chance to spot seals, dolphins, and a variety of seabirds. Sea kayaking around the Isle of Skye provides a unique perspective on the island's rugged coastline, with its towering sea cliffs and hidden coves. Guided sea kayaking tours are available for those seeking expert instruction and local knowledge, ensuring a safe and enriching experience.

For thrill-seekers, coasteering provides an exhilarating way to explore Scotland's coastal landscapes. This adventure activity involves scrambling, swimming, and jumping along the rocky coastline, navigating through sea caves and over tidal pools. The east coast, particularly around St. Andrews and the East Neuk of Fife, offers excellent coasteering opportunities, with its sandstone cliffs and hidden beaches. Coasteering is typically done with a guide, providing both safety and expertise in navigating the challenging terrain. It's a high-energy activity that combines elements of rock climbing, swimming, and exploration, offering an unforgettable way to experience Scotland's coastline.

Scotland's rivers also provide excellent opportunities for canyoning, an adventure sport that involves descending through river gorges using a combination of walking, scrambling, abseiling, and swimming. The Cairngorms National Park is home to some of Scotland's best canyoning locations, with the Bruar and Dollar canyons offering thrilling descents through waterfalls and natural rock slides. Canyoning tours are available for different skill levels, from beginner routes with gentle slides and jumps to more challenging adventures that require technical skills and confidence. The combination of adrenaline and natural beauty makes canyoning a popular choice for those seeking an adventurous day out.

For a more tranquil water-based activity, fishing in Scotland offers a chance to relax and connect with nature while pursuing one of the country's most treasured pastimes. Scotland is renowned for its salmon and trout fishing, with rivers such as the Spey, Tay, and Dee offering world-class angling opportunities. Fly fishing is the most popular method, with anglers casting their lines in the hope of landing a prized salmon or trout. Many fishing lodges and outfitters offer guided fishing trips, providing equipment, instruction, and local knowledge to help anglers make the most of their fishing experience. Scotland's lochs also offer excellent fishing opportunities, with pike, perch, and brown trout among the species commonly found.

Scotland's coastal waters provide opportunities for diving, with numerous shipwrecks and marine life to explore. The Orkney Islands, particularly Scapa Flow, are renowned for their dive sites, with the remains of the German High Seas Fleet from World War I resting on the seabed. These historic wrecks attract divers from around the world, offering a unique glimpse into maritime history. The clear waters and abundant marine life, including seals and colorful anemones, make Orkney a top diving destination. Diving courses and guided trips are available for divers of all levels, ensuring a safe and memorable underwater adventure.

For those interested in sailing, Scotland's west coast offers some of the best cruising grounds in the world, with its sheltered waters, stunning scenery, and numerous islands to explore. The Firth of Clyde, with its mix of open water and sheltered bays, is a popular destination for sailors, offering a variety of anchorages and marinas. The Inner Hebrides, including the islands of Mull, Jura, and Islay, provide a picturesque backdrop for a sailing adventure, with opportunities to explore charming coastal villages, historic castles, and whisky distilleries along the way. Sailing schools and charter companies offer lessons and boat rentals, catering to both seasoned sailors and those new to the sport.

When participating in water sports in Scotland, it's important to be prepared for the country's variable weather conditions. Even in summer, the water can be cold, so appropriate clothing such as wetsuits and waterproof gear is essential. Safety should always be a priority, with participants ensuring they have the necessary skills, equipment, and local knowledge for their chosen activity. Whether you're seeking the thrill of surfing, the tranquility of kayaking, or the adventure of coasteering, Scotland's diverse water sports and activities offer something for everyone.

Scotland's water-based adventures invite exploration and discovery, offering a unique perspective on the country's landscapes and wildlife. The blend of natural beauty, cultural heritage, and outdoor adventure creates an experience that is truly unforgettable. Whether navigating the waves, paddling serene lochs, or exploring underwater worlds, each water sport offers a connection to Scotland's natural environment and a chance to create lasting memories in one of the world's most captivating destinations.

Golf Courses and Clubs

Scotland, often hailed as the birthplace of golf, offers an unparalleled experience for enthusiasts seeking to immerse themselves in the sport's rich history and tradition. With its rolling landscapes, historic courses, and welcoming clubs, Scotland provides a golfing journey that is both nostalgic and invigorating. Whether you're a seasoned player or a newcomer to the game, the country's golf courses and clubs offer a diverse range of experiences that cater to all skill levels.

St. Andrews, known as the "Home of Golf," is a pilgrimage for golfers from around the globe. The Old Course, with its iconic Swilcan Bridge and Hell Bunker, is steeped in history and tradition, offering golfers the chance to walk in the footsteps of legends. Playing a round at the Old Course is both a challenge and an honor, with its undulating fairways and unpredictable coastal winds testing even the most skilled players. For those unable to secure a tee time, the St. Andrews Links Trust manages several other courses, including the New Course and the Castle Course, each offering its unique blend of history and modern design.

The Royal and Ancient Golf Club of St. Andrews, founded in 1754, is one of the world's oldest and most prestigious golf clubs, serving as a governing body for the sport. While membership is exclusive, the club's influence on the game is profound, contributing to the development of rules and standards that have shaped modern golf. Visitors to St. Andrews can explore the British Golf Museum, located near the Old Course, to gain insight into the history and evolution of the game.

Beyond St. Andrews, Scotland boasts a wealth of world-class courses, each with its own character and charm. Royal Troon, located on the west coast, has hosted numerous Open Championships and is known for its challenging layout and stunning coastal views. The course's famous "Postage Stamp" hole, a par three with a small green and challenging bunkers, is a favorite among players and spectators alike. The club's rich history and championship pedigree make it a must-visit destination for golf aficionados.

Muirfield, another prestigious venue, is home to the Honourable Company of Edinburgh Golfers, one of the oldest golf clubs in the world. The course is renowned for its strategic design and immaculate condition, offering a true test of skill and strategy. Muirfield has hosted numerous major championships, including the Open, and is revered for its traditional approach to the game. Visitors to Muirfield are greeted with a warm Scottish welcome, and the opportunity to play this historic course is a highlight for many golfers.

For those seeking a more contemporary golfing experience, the Gleneagles Resort offers three championship courses set amidst the stunning Perthshire countryside. The PGA Centenary Course, designed by Jack Nicklaus, hosted the 2014 Ryder Cup and is known for its challenging layout and breathtaking views. The King's and Queen's Courses, designed by James Braid, offer a more traditional golfing experience, with their natural contours and strategic bunkering. Gleneagles provides a complete golfing experience, with luxurious accommodations, fine dining, and a range of leisure activities.

Scotland's links courses, characterized by their coastal locations, natural terrain, and challenging conditions, offer a quintessential golfing experience. Royal Dornoch, located in the Highlands, is a classic links course with stunning views of the Dornoch Firth. Its remote location adds to its charm, offering a peaceful escape for golfers seeking to connect with nature. The course's unique design, with its raised greens and deep bunkers, provides a challenging yet rewarding experience.

The Machrihanish Golf Club, situated on the Kintyre Peninsula, is another hidden gem. Known for its stunning opening hole, which requires a drive across the Atlantic Ocean, Machrihanish offers a true links experience with its natural dunes and panoramic views. The course's remote location adds to its allure, making it a favorite among those seeking an authentic and unspoiled golfing adventure.

For beginners or those looking to improve their skills, Scotland offers numerous golf academies and practice facilities. The St. Andrews Links Academy provides world-class instruction with its state-of-the-art facilities and experienced coaches. Players can benefit from personalized coaching, practice on dedicated short-game areas, and utilize cutting-edge technology to analyze their swing and improve their game. These facilities offer golfers of all levels the opportunity to refine their skills and gain confidence on the course.

Scottish golf clubs are known for their welcoming atmosphere and sense of camaraderie, with many offering opportunities to engage with local members and participate in club events. The game of golf is deeply ingrained in Scottish culture, and visitors can expect a warm reception and a genuine passion for the sport. Whether enjoying a post-round drink in the clubhouse or sharing stories on the course, the social aspect of golf in Scotland is an integral part of the experience.

When planning a golf trip to Scotland, it's important to consider the country's variable weather conditions. Layers of clothing, waterproof gear, and sturdy footwear are essential for staying comfortable on the course. Many courses offer caddies, who provide invaluable local knowledge and assistance, enhancing the overall experience. Booking tee times in advance is recommended, especially for the more popular courses, to ensure a seamless and enjoyable golfing adventure.

Golfing in Scotland is more than just a game; it's an immersion into the history and tradition of a sport that has captivated players for centuries. Each course tells a story, offering a unique blend of challenge and beauty that invites golfers to test their skills and create lasting memories. Whether navigating the legendary links of St. Andrews, discovering hidden gems along the coast, or honing skills at a world-class academy, Scotland's golf courses and clubs offer an unforgettable journey into the heart of the game.

Wildlife Watching and Eco-Tours

Scotland's diverse ecosystems and breathtaking landscapes provide a sanctuary for a wide array of wildlife, making it a prime destination for nature enthusiasts and eco-tourists. From the rugged Highlands to the serene islands, the country offers numerous opportunities to observe its rich biodiversity in their natural habitats. Whether you're interested in spotting majestic birds of prey, witnessing marine life in their coastal havens, or exploring the flora and fauna of ancient woodlands, Scotland's wildlife watching experiences promise unforgettable encounters with nature.

The Cairngorms National Park, the largest national park in the UK, is a haven for wildlife and a must-visit for any nature lover. Home to some of the country's most iconic species, the park offers a chance to see the elusive Scottish wildcat, red deer, and the rare capercaillie. The vast expanse of the park, with its diverse habitats ranging from ancient Caledonian pine forests to open moorlands, provides a rich environment for wildlife to thrive. Bird watchers will be delighted by the presence of the golden eagle and the osprey, both of which can be spotted soaring above the rugged terrain in search of prey. Guided wildlife tours, led by knowledgeable local experts, offer visitors the opportunity to explore the park's hidden corners and learn about its unique ecosystems.

Scotland's islands also boast an impressive array of wildlife, with the Outer Hebrides being a particularly rewarding destination for wildlife enthusiasts. The islands are home to large colonies of seabirds, including puffins, guillemots, and razorbills. The cliffs of St. Kilda, a UNESCO World Heritage Site, provide a dramatic backdrop for observing these seabirds in their natural environment. The islands' coastal waters are inhabited by seals, dolphins, and even whales, offering thrilling opportunities for marine wildlife watching. Boat tours around the islands provide a chance to see these creatures up close, with experienced guides providing insights into their behavior and ecology.

The Isle of Mull, with its rugged coastline and diverse habitats, is renowned for its wildlife watching opportunities. The island is one of the best places in the UK to see white-tailed eagles, the largest bird of prey in the country. These magnificent birds can often be seen soaring above the island's lochs and cliffs, providing a breathtaking sight for visitors. Mull is also home to otters, red deer, and a variety of bird species, making it a rich destination for nature lovers. Guided wildlife tours on the island offer the chance to explore its hidden gems and learn about the conservation efforts in place to protect its unique biodiversity.

The Scottish Highlands, with their dramatic landscapes and remote beauty, offer a chance to encounter some of the country's most iconic wildlife. Red deer, often referred to as the "Monarch of the Glen," can be seen roaming the hills and glens, particularly during the autumn rutting season when the males engage in dramatic displays of strength and dominance. The Highlands are also home to the elusive pine marten and the charming red squirrel, both of which can be spotted in the region's ancient woodlands. Wildlife safaris, led by experienced guides, offer the opportunity to explore these remote landscapes and observe their inhabitants in their natural surroundings.

Scotland's coastal waters are teeming with marine life, making them a prime destination for eco-tours and wildlife watching trips. The Moray Firth, located in the northeast of Scotland, is home to a resident population of bottlenose dolphins, which can often be seen leaping and playing in the waters. Boat tours departing from towns like Inverness and Cromarty provide the chance to see these dolphins up close, with experienced guides offering insights into their behavior and ecology. The Firth of Forth, near Edinburgh, is another excellent location for marine wildlife watching, with opportunities to see seals, porpoises, and a variety of seabirds.

The conservation of Scotland's wildlife and natural habitats is a priority for many organizations and communities, and eco-tours provide an opportunity to learn about and support these efforts. Many wildlife tours and experiences in Scotland are operated by organizations committed to sustainable tourism and conservation, ensuring that visitors can enjoy the country's natural beauty while contributing to its preservation.

These tours often include educational components, providing insights into the challenges faced by Scotland's wildlife and the measures being taken to protect them.

For those interested in botany, Scotland's diverse plant life offers a rich field of exploration. The country's ancient woodlands, such as the Caledonian Forest, are home to a variety of native plant species, including Scots pine, juniper, and a wealth of mosses and lichens. The machair, a unique coastal grassland found in the Hebrides, is renowned for its vibrant display of wildflowers during the summer months. Guided botanical tours provide the chance to learn about Scotland's unique plant species and their ecological importance, offering a deeper understanding of the country's natural heritage.

When embarking on wildlife watching and eco-tours in Scotland, it's important to be prepared for the country's variable weather conditions. Layered clothing, waterproof gear, and sturdy footwear are essential for staying comfortable during outdoor excursions. Binoculars and cameras are also recommended for capturing the beauty of Scotland's wildlife and landscapes. Visitors should be respectful of the natural environment and adhere to the Scottish Outdoor Access Code, ensuring that their activities do not disturb the wildlife or their habitats.

Scotland's wildlife watching and eco-tour experiences offer a unique opportunity to connect with nature and explore the country's rich biodiversity. From the soaring eagles of the Highlands to the playful dolphins of the Moray Firth, each encounter provides a glimpse into the beauty and wonder of Scotland's natural world. Whether exploring remote islands, ancient forests, or coastal waters, visitors are invited to discover the magic of Scotland's wildlife and contribute to the conservation of its precious ecosystems.

CHAPTER 8: PRACTICAL TRAVEL TIPS

Navigating Public Transport

Navigating public transport in Scotland offers travelers a convenient and often scenic way to explore the country's diverse landscapes and cultural landmarks. From the bustling streets of Edinburgh to the remote beauty of the Highlands, Scotland's public transport network provides a reliable and efficient means of getting around. Understanding how to utilize trains, buses, ferries, and even bicycles for urban and rural travel can greatly enhance your Scottish adventure.

Scotland's rail network is an excellent option for exploring the country, with services operated primarily by ScotRail. The train system connects major cities, towns, and numerous picturesque destinations, making it an ideal choice for both short commutes and longer journeys. The scenic routes, such as the West Highland Line, offer breathtaking views of lochs, mountains, and glens, providing an unforgettable travel experience. Booking train tickets in advance can secure better fares, especially for popular routes. Travelers can purchase tickets online, at stations, or using mobile apps, which also provide real-time updates on schedules and delays.

For those planning to explore multiple destinations, the Spirit of Scotland Travelpass offers unlimited travel on the rail network for a set number of days. This pass can be particularly useful for visitors seeking to cover a lot of ground in a short period. Another option is the BritRail Freedom of Scotland Pass, which also includes some ferry services, providing flexibility for those venturing to Scotland's islands.

Scotland's bus network complements the rail system, reaching areas that trains might not. Intercity and regional bus services are operated by companies such as Citylink and Stagecoach, providing connections to towns and rural areas. Buses are often the best choice for accessing remote locations and smaller communities, offering a cost-effective way to explore the country. Tickets can be purchased in advance or directly from the driver, and mobile apps can assist with planning routes and checking schedules.

For local travel within cities, buses offer an efficient means of navigating urban areas. Edinburgh and Glasgow have extensive bus networks, with frequent services and multiple routes covering the cities and suburbs. Day tickets and contactless payment options make it easy for travelers to hop on and off buses as they explore. In Glasgow, the subway system, known as the "Clockwork Orange," provides a quick and convenient way to travel around the city center, with a circular route that connects key locations.

Ferries are an essential part of Scotland's transport network, particularly for reaching the islands scattered along the west coast. Caledonian MacBrayne, known as CalMac, operates the majority of ferry services, connecting the mainland to the Inner and Outer Hebrides. Ferries vary in size and frequency, depending on the route, and it's advisable to book tickets in advance, especially during peak travel seasons. The ferry journeys themselves often offer spectacular views of the coastline and are an integral part of the Scottish travel experience.

For those planning to explore the islands extensively, the Island Hopscotch ticket offers a flexible travel option, allowing travelers to visit multiple islands on a single ticket. This can be a cost-effective way to explore the unique landscapes and cultures of Scotland's island communities.

Cycling is a popular way to explore Scotland, with many towns and cities offering bike rental services and dedicated cycling paths. Urban bike-share schemes, such as those in Glasgow and Edinburgh, provide an eco-friendly and enjoyable way to navigate city streets. Scotland's National Cycle Network offers a range of routes for cyclists of all abilities, allowing for exploration of both urban areas and picturesque countryside.

When using public transport in Scotland, it's important to be mindful of the country's weather conditions, which can be unpredictable. Dress in layers and carry waterproof clothing to stay comfortable during your travels. Many public transport options offer free Wi-Fi, allowing travelers to stay connected and access travel information on the go.

For those new to using public transport in Scotland, local staff and information centers can provide valuable assistance. Transport hubs such as train stations and bus terminals often have information desks where travelers can seek advice, collect maps, and obtain schedules. Friendly locals are also usually willing to offer directions and recommendations, adding to the warm and welcoming experience of traveling in Scotland.

Understanding the cultural nuances of using public transport in Scotland can enhance your journey. It's customary to greet the driver when boarding a bus and to thank them when disembarking. Offering your seat to elderly passengers or those with disabilities is also appreciated. In trains and buses, keeping noise to a minimum and respecting personal space ensures a pleasant journey for all passengers.

Incorporating public transport into your travel plans allows for a more sustainable approach to exploring Scotland. Reducing the reliance on cars helps minimize the environmental impact of travel, aligning with Scotland's commitment to sustainability and conservation. Additionally, public transport provides a unique opportunity to experience the country from a local perspective, offering insights into daily life and the chance to interact with fellow travelers and residents.

Traveling by public transport in Scotland opens up a world of possibilities, from the vibrant energy of its cities to the tranquil beauty of its rural landscapes. The convenience and accessibility of the transport network make it easy for travelers to discover the country's hidden gems and iconic landmarks. Whether you're savoring the scenic views from a train window, navigating the charming streets of a historic town by bus, or embarking on a ferry journey to a distant island, Scotland's public transport system invites you to explore its rich tapestry of experiences.

Accommodation Options for Every Budget

Finding the right accommodation is a crucial part of planning a trip to Scotland, ensuring comfort and convenience while complementing the overall travel experience. The country offers a diverse array of lodging options that cater to every budget, from luxurious castles and boutique hotels to quaint bed and breakfasts and budget-friendly hostels. Understanding these options can help travelers make informed choices that suit their preferences and enhance their Scottish adventure.

For those seeking luxury and elegance, Scotland's historic castles and manor houses provide a unique and opulent experience. Many of these estates have been converted into luxury hotels, offering guests the chance to immerse themselves in Scotland's rich history and heritage. With their grand architecture, manicured gardens, and lavish interiors, these accommodations provide a regal atmosphere and exceptional service. Properties such as Inverlochy Castle Hotel near Fort William and Glenapp Castle in Ayrshire offer a blend of historical charm and modern amenities, ensuring a memorable stay. Guests can enjoy fine dining, spa treatments, and activities such as golf and falconry, making for a truly indulgent experience.

Boutique hotels are another excellent option for travelers seeking a more personalized and intimate stay. These hotels often reflect the unique character of their location, offering stylish design and thoughtful amenities. Many boutique hotels are independently owned, providing a warm and welcoming atmosphere with exceptional attention to detail. In Edinburgh, the Witchery by the Castle offers a gothic-inspired experience with its opulent rooms and candlelit dining, while the Kimpton Blythswood Square Hotel in Glasgow combines contemporary luxury with historic elegance.

For those who prefer a more traditional Scottish experience, bed and breakfasts (B&Bs) offer a cozy and authentic option. B&Bs are typically family-run, providing a warm and friendly environment with personalized service. Guests can enjoy home-cooked breakfasts featuring local produce, and hosts often provide valuable insights and tips for exploring the area. B&Bs are found throughout Scotland, from bustling cities to remote villages, offering a range of styles and prices to suit different preferences. Staying at a B&B allows travelers to connect with local culture and gain a deeper understanding of the region's traditions and way of life.

Self-catering accommodations such as cottages, apartments, and holiday homes offer flexibility and independence, making them a popular choice for families and groups. These accommodations provide the convenience of a home-away-from-home, with fully equipped kitchens and living spaces. Self-catering options are available in a variety of settings, from city centers to rural retreats, allowing travelers to tailor their stay to their interests. Renting a cottage in the Highlands or on one of Scotland's islands offers the opportunity to enjoy stunning natural surroundings and engage in outdoor activities at your own pace. Many self-catering properties are pet-friendly, making them an excellent choice for travelers with pets.

For budget-conscious travelers, hostels offer affordable and sociable accommodation options. Hostels in Scotland range from modern urban facilities to rustic rural lodges, providing a variety of experiences. Many hostels offer private rooms as well as dormitory-style accommodation, catering to different needs and preferences. Hostels are a great way to meet fellow travelers and share experiences, with communal areas such as kitchens and lounges fostering a sense of community. The Scottish Youth Hostels Association (SYHA) operates hostels in key locations across the country, offering reliable and budget-friendly options for exploring Scotland.

Camping and glamping provide a closer connection to Scotland's natural landscapes, offering an adventurous and immersive experience. Traditional campsites are available throughout the country, providing basic facilities and the opportunity to enjoy the great outdoors. For a more comfortable and unique camping experience, glamping sites offer stylish accommodations such as yurts, pods, and safari tents, often with added amenities like electricity and private bathrooms. Glamping allows travelers to enjoy the beauty of Scotland's countryside while maintaining a level of comfort and convenience.

When choosing accommodations in Scotland, it's important to consider factors such as location, amenities, and accessibility. Proximity to public transport, attractions, and dining options can greatly enhance the convenience and enjoyment of your stay. Many accommodations offer online booking, allowing travelers to compare prices, read reviews, and secure their preferred lodging in advance. During peak travel seasons and popular events, booking early is advisable to ensure availability and secure the best rates.

Scotland's diverse accommodation options reflect the country's unique blend of history, culture, and natural beauty, offering something for every traveler. Whether you're seeking the grandeur of a castle, the charm of a bed and breakfast, the flexibility of self-catering, or the adventure of camping, Scotland provides a range of choices to suit every budget and preference. Each accommodation type offers its own distinct experience, inviting travelers to discover the warmth and hospitality that Scotland is renowned for.

Exploring the various accommodation options in Scotland allows travelers to tailor their journey to their unique interests and needs, creating a personalized and memorable travel experience. Whether you're embarking on a solo adventure, a romantic getaway, or a family vacation, the right lodging choice can enhance your Scottish adventure and provide a comfortable base from which to explore the country's rich tapestry of landscapes and cultural treasures.

Safety and Emergency Information

Traveling in Scotland offers breathtaking landscapes and vibrant culture, but being informed about safety and emergency protocols ensures a worry-free experience. Understanding the nuances of safety in various settings, from bustling urban centers to remote rural areas, equips travelers with the confidence to explore with peace of mind.

Urban safety in Scotland's major cities, such as Edinburgh and Glasgow, is comparable to other European destinations. These cities boast low crime rates, but it's important to remain vigilant, particularly in crowded areas. Pickpocketing can occur in tourist hotspots, so keeping personal belongings secure is advisable. Utilizing crossbody bags, money belts, and keeping valuables close helps deter opportunistic theft. When withdrawing cash, using ATMs located inside banks reduces the risk of card skimming or theft.

Public transportation in Scotland is generally safe and reliable. Late-night travelers should opt for the front carriages of trains and buses, closer to the driver. When using taxis, it's recommended to choose licensed operators, easily identified by their official signage. Ride-hailing apps provide a convenient and secure alternative, allowing passengers to verify the driver's identity and track the journey.

Rural areas and natural landscapes in Scotland require specific precautions. Weather conditions can change rapidly, especially in the Highlands and coastal regions. Packing appropriate gear such as waterproof clothing, sturdy footwear, and layers helps ensure comfort and safety during outdoor excursions. Informing someone of your itinerary, especially when hiking or engaging in remote activities, enhances safety.

Mobile phone reception can be unreliable in remote areas, so carrying a paper map and compass can be invaluable.

Wildlife encounters, while often a highlight of Scottish travel, necessitate caution. Observing animals from a safe distance and avoiding feeding or approaching them is crucial to both personal safety and the preservation of natural behaviors. Insect repellent is advisable, particularly in summer months when midges are prevalent in certain regions.

For those driving in Scotland, understanding road safety is essential. Roads can be narrow and winding, especially in rural areas, where visibility is reduced due to weather conditions or natural obstacles. Adhering to speed limits and road signs ensures safe navigation. Single-track roads, common in the Highlands and islands, require awareness of passing places to allow oncoming traffic to pass safely. It's important to drive on the left side of the road and familiarize oneself with roundabouts, which are frequent on Scottish roads.

Emergency services in Scotland are efficient and accessible. The emergency number for police, fire, and ambulance services is 999. In non-emergency situations, the police can be reached at 101, offering assistance with non-urgent issues.

Familiarizing yourself with the location of the nearest hospital or medical facility is prudent, especially for those with specific health concerns. Pharmacies are widely available in cities and towns, providing both medications and health advice.

Travel insurance is a vital component of trip planning, offering protection against unforeseen events such as medical emergencies, trip cancellations, or lost belongings. Ensuring that the policy covers activities planned, such as hiking or adventure sports, provides an added layer of security. Keeping a copy of the insurance policy and emergency contact numbers easily accessible is wise.

Cultural awareness enhances safety and enriches the travel experience. Understanding local customs and etiquette fosters positive interactions and helps avoid misunderstandings. For instance, in rural areas, closing gates behind you when walking through farmland is a common courtesy. Additionally, respecting private property and following designated paths helps maintain good relations with local communities.

The weather can be unpredictable, with sudden changes common, particularly in mountainous regions. Checking weather forecasts regularly and being prepared for rapid shifts in conditions is crucial. In winter months, snow and ice may impact travel plans, requiring flexibility and the use of appropriate transport or accommodations.

Travelers with specific needs or disabilities will find Scotland increasingly accessible, with many transport services and attractions offering facilities such as ramps, lifts, and accessible restrooms. Inquiring about accessibility in advance ensures a smoother experience. The VisitScotland website provides information on accessible travel and accommodations, helping travelers plan their journey with confidence.

For those who may require legal assistance or face consular issues, embassies and consulates in Scotland can provide support. Keeping a record of the nearest consulate's contact details is prudent, particularly for travelers from outside the UK. They can assist with lost passports, legal matters, and other emergencies.

In terms of health, Scotland offers high-quality medical care through the National Health Service (NHS), which provides treatment for emergencies. Travelers from the European Union, with an EHIC card, and those from countries with reciprocal healthcare agreements may access certain services.

However, comprehensive travel insurance remains essential to cover any additional medical expenses.

Being informed and prepared enhances the enjoyment of Scotland's diverse offerings while ensuring safety and readiness for any situation. From the vibrant cityscapes to the serene wilderness, Scotland invites exploration and discovery, with the assurance that safety and emergency services are robust and effective. Whether admiring the historic streets of Edinburgh or the dramatic landscapes of Skye, a well-prepared traveler can fully embrace the richness and beauty of a Scottish adventure.

Essential Packing Tips

Preparing for a trip to Scotland involves more than just booking flights and accommodations. The country's diverse climates and range of activities require thoughtful packing to ensure a comfortable and enjoyable experience. From the bustling cities to the tranquil countryside, each destination presents its own unique demands on your wardrobe and gear. Understanding what to bring and how to pack efficiently will help you make the most of your Scottish adventure.

Scotland's weather is famously unpredictable, with conditions that can change rapidly, even within a single day. This makes layering your clothing an essential strategy. Start with a moisture-wicking base layer, which helps regulate body temperature and keeps you dry during physical activities. On top of this, add an insulating layer such as a fleece or wool sweater for warmth. Finally, a waterproof and windproof outer shell will protect you from rain and blustery winds, both of which are common throughout the country.

Footwear is another critical consideration, especially if you plan to explore the great outdoors. A sturdy pair of waterproof hiking boots is indispensable for tackling Scotland's rugged terrains, from the Highlands' steep trails to the coastal paths of the islands. For city exploration, comfortable walking shoes are a must, as cobblestone streets and historic sites often require extensive walking.

The right accessories can make a significant difference in your comfort and convenience while traveling. A wide-brimmed hat or a cap provides protection from both rain and sun, while a pair of sunglasses with UV protection shields your eyes from glare. Don't forget a reliable travel umbrella, which can be a lifesaver in sudden downpours. Additionally, gloves and a warm scarf are advisable during the colder months, providing extra warmth on chilly days.

Packing smart also means being prepared for different activities and occasions. If you plan to dine in some of Scotland's finer establishments or attend cultural events, bringing a set of smart-casual clothing is wise. A pair of dress shoes, a collared shirt or blouse, and tailored trousers or a nice dress can easily elevate your appearance for more formal settings. For those interested in outdoor activities, such as cycling or kayaking, quick-drying sportswear and swimwear should be included.

Toiletries and medications are another area where careful planning is essential. While most essentials can be purchased in Scotland, it's wise to bring a supply of your favorite personal care products, especially if you have specific preferences or allergies. Travel-sized containers are ideal for packing liquids, and a clear, resealable bag will keep them organized and compliant with airport security regulations. If you take prescription medications, ensure you have enough for the duration of your trip, along with a copy of the prescription in case you need a refill.

Technology plays a crucial role in modern travel, and bringing the right gadgets can enhance your experience. A universal power adapter is necessary for charging electronic devices, as Scotland uses the UK-type plug with three rectangular pins. A portable charger is also invaluable for keeping your phone and other devices powered during long days of exploration. If you plan to document your journey, a good-quality camera or smartphone with ample storage and a reliable case for protection is essential.

Staying organized while traveling can reduce stress and make navigating through airports and accommodations smoother. Packing cubes or compression bags are excellent tools for maximizing suitcase space and keeping clothing organized. A travel-sized laundry kit, including detergent and a clothesline, can be useful for refreshing your wardrobe during longer trips. A lightweight daypack or backpack is ideal for carrying daily essentials, such as a water bottle, snacks, and a map or guidebook, while exploring.

While it's important to be prepared, overpacking can be cumbersome. Prioritize versatile clothing items that can be mixed and matched to create different outfits. Choose fabrics that resist wrinkles and can be layered comfortably. Remember that most accommodations offer laundry facilities, allowing you to refresh your wardrobe without carrying excessive luggage.

Scotland's natural beauty and cultural richness offer endless opportunities for exploration, and being well-prepared with the right gear enhances these experiences. Packing thoughtfully not only ensures comfort but also allows you to adapt to the country's varied climates and activities with ease. From the serene lochs and majestic castles to the vibrant cityscapes, having the essentials on hand lets you fully immerse yourself in all that Scotland has to offer.

As you prepare for your journey, consider the environmental impact of your packing choices. Opt for reusable items, such as a water bottle and shopping tote, to minimize waste. Choosing eco-friendly toiletries and clothing made from sustainable materials can also contribute to more responsible travel. By packing with intention and awareness, you can enjoy the wonders of Scotland while respecting its natural and cultural heritage.

Ultimately, the key to successful packing lies in balance— bringing enough to cover your needs while maintaining the flexibility to adapt to Scotland's dynamic environment. Whether you're embarking on a hike through the Highlands, exploring the historic streets of Edinburgh, or savoring the tranquility of the islands, being well-prepared ensures a seamless and memorable adventure.

CHAPTER 9: UNIQUE EXPERIENCES AND OFF-THE-BEATEN-PATH

Hidden Villages and Towns

Scotland, renowned for its dramatic landscapes and rich history, is also home to numerous hidden villages and towns that offer a unique glimpse into the country's lesser-known treasures. These charming locales, tucked away from the usual tourist trails, provide an authentic experience of Scottish culture, history, and hospitality. Exploring these hidden gems can reveal a different side of Scotland, where time moves at a gentler pace, and the stories of the past echo through cobbled streets and ancient ruins.

Nestled in the heart of the Cairngorms National Park lies Braemar, a picturesque village renowned for its breathtaking scenery and historic charm. Surrounded by towering mountains and lush forests, Braemar is a haven for outdoor enthusiasts, offering activities such as hiking, mountain biking, and skiing. The village is famous for hosting the Braemar Gathering, a traditional Highland Games event that attracts visitors from around the world. With its friendly locals and vibrant community spirit, Braemar embodies the essence of Scottish village life.

Further north, the village of Pennan clings to the rugged cliffs of the Aberdeenshire coast. This tiny fishing village gained fame as a filming location for the classic film "Local Hero," and its iconic red phone box has become a symbol of its quaint charm. Pennan's whitewashed cottages and narrow lanes create a sense of stepping back in time, offering a peaceful retreat from the hustle and bustle of modern life. The village's coastal setting provides opportunities for exploring nearby beaches and enjoying fresh seafood from local eateries.

In the rolling hills of the Scottish Borders, the town of Melrose invites visitors to explore its rich history and cultural heritage. Melrose Abbey, a stunning medieval ruin, stands as a testament to the town's historical significance, believed to be the burial site of Robert the Bruce's heart. The town's vibrant arts scene, charming boutiques, and cozy cafes create a welcoming atmosphere for travelers seeking a blend of history and modernity. The annual Melrose Sevens, a rugby sevens tournament, adds to the town's lively character and draws sports enthusiasts from near and far.

On the Isle of Mull, the village of Tobermory captivates visitors with its colorful waterfront and lively atmosphere. Known for its brightly painted buildings lining the harbor, Tobermory offers a unique blend of natural beauty and cultural experiences. The village is home to a distillery producing the renowned Tobermory whisky, providing an opportunity for visitors to sample local flavors and learn about the art of whisky-making. The surrounding landscapes offer adventures in wildlife watching, with opportunities to spot otters, seals, and even whales along the coast.

The village of Plockton, situated on the shores of Loch Carron, is often referred to as the "Jewel of the Highlands." Its palm-lined streets, a result of the Gulf Stream's warming influence, create a unique microclimate that sets it apart from typical Highland scenery. Plockton's stunning vistas and tranquil setting make it a popular destination for artists and photographers seeking inspiration. The village's seafood restaurants serve some of the freshest catches in Scotland, offering visitors a true taste of the sea.

In the far north, the village of Durness offers a remote and rugged beauty that captivates the adventurous traveler. With its dramatic cliffs, pristine beaches, and turquoise waters, Durness is a paradise for nature lovers. The nearby Smoo Cave, a large sea cave, is a geological wonder waiting to be explored. Durness is also home to a vibrant arts community, with local galleries showcasing the work of talented artists inspired by the area's natural beauty.

In exploring these hidden villages and towns, visitors often find that the journey itself is as rewarding as the destination. Winding roads lead through breathtaking landscapes, unveiling panoramic vistas and hidden corners of natural beauty. Along the way, encounters with friendly locals provide insights into the traditions and stories that shape these communities. Whether it's sharing a conversation over a pint in a village pub or learning about local crafts from an artisan, these interactions enrich the travel experience and create lasting memories.

Discovering Scotland's hidden villages and towns offers a chance to connect with the country's soul, away from the well-trodden paths of major tourist destinations. Each village and town holds its own unique charm and character, inviting travelers to slow down and savor the simple pleasures of life. Whether you're drawn to the rugged coastlines, the rolling hills, or the majestic mountains, Scotland's off-the-beaten-path locales promise an adventure filled with wonder and discovery.

These hidden gems are a testament to Scotland's diversity, offering a tapestry of experiences that reflect the country's rich cultural heritage and stunning natural landscapes. By venturing beyond the familiar, travelers can uncover the true essence of Scotland, where every village and town has a story to tell and a warm welcome to offer. Embracing the spirit of exploration and curiosity, these lesser-known destinations invite you to embark on a journey of discovery, where the beauty of Scotland's hidden corners unfolds before your eyes.

Unique Accommodations

Scotland's unique accommodations offer an extraordinary opportunity to experience the country in ways that go beyond traditional hotels and guesthouses. From historic castles and remote bothies to eco-friendly hideaways and floating lodges, these distinctive lodgings provide immersive encounters with Scotland's rich heritage and breathtaking landscapes. Each offers a unique blend of comfort, adventure, and cultural connection, inviting travelers to explore the country's storied past and natural beauty from a fresh perspective.

Staying in a Scottish castle is a dream come true for many visitors, a chance to step into a world of grandeur and history. These castles, often dating back centuries, have been meticulously restored to offer modern comforts while preserving their historical charm. Guests can wander through grand halls, sleep in turreted bedrooms, and dine in opulent banquet rooms. Castles like Inverlochy Castle in the Highlands and Dalhousie Castle near Edinburgh offer luxurious experiences with gourmet dining, spa treatments, and activities such as falconry and archery. The sense of history and romance that permeates these walls is palpable, making a castle stay an unforgettable experience.

For those seeking solitude and a connection with the rugged Scottish landscape, bothies provide a unique and rustic accommodation option. These simple shelters, scattered across remote areas, were once used by shepherds and travelers. Today, they offer refuge for hikers and adventurers exploring Scotland's expansive wilderness. Bothies are typically basic, with no electricity or running water, and guests are encouraged to follow a leave-no-trace ethos. Staying in a bothy allows for a profound sense of isolation and tranquility, with the opportunity to witness stunning sunrises and sunsets over unspoiled landscapes.

Eco-friendly accommodations are becoming increasingly popular in Scotland, reflecting a growing commitment to sustainable tourism. These lodgings are designed to minimize environmental impact while offering comfort and luxury. The EcoYoga Centre in Argyll combines eco-conscious design with wellness, offering yoga retreats in a serene natural setting. The center uses renewable energy sources and provides guests with organic, locally-sourced meals. Similarly, the Loch

Ossian Youth Hostel, accessible only by foot or bicycle, is powered by wind and solar energy, providing a truly off-grid experience amidst the beauty of the Highlands.

For a truly unique experience, floating lodges offer a distinctive way to stay close to Scotland's waterways. These accommodations, often moored on lochs or rivers, provide panoramic views and a sense of serenity. Guests can enjoy activities such as fishing, kayaking, or simply relaxing on the deck while taking in the tranquil scenery. The Anchor Belle Houseboat on Loch Fyne offers a luxurious floating stay with modern amenities and easy access to the surrounding natural attractions. Floating lodges blend the novelty of staying on water with the comforts of home, creating an unforgettable experience.

The concept of glamping—glamorous camping—has taken root in Scotland, offering a way to experience the great outdoors with added comfort and style. Glamping sites range from safari tents and yurts to treehouses and geodesic domes, often situated in picturesque locations. These accommodations provide cozy interiors with comfortable beds, heating, and sometimes en-suite facilities. Glamping allows travelers to enjoy the beauty of Scotland's landscapes without sacrificing comfort, making it an ideal option for families or those new to camping.

Lighthouses, iconic symbols of Scotland's maritime heritage, have been converted into unique accommodations, offering panoramic views and a sense of adventure. Staying in a lighthouse provides a glimpse into the life of a lighthouse keeper, with the constant sound of the sea and sweeping views of the coastline. The Corsewall Lighthouse Hotel in Dumfries and Galloway offers a luxurious stay with elegantly appointed rooms and gourmet dining, all within the historic lighthouse tower. The experience of climbing to the top of the lighthouse for a sunset view is truly magical.

For those interested in Scotland's cultural heritage, traditional crofts—small agricultural holdings—offer a unique accommodation experience. These self-catering cottages, often located in rural or island settings, provide insight into Scotland's agricultural past and a chance to experience traditional Highland life. Staying in a croft allows guests to engage with local communities, learn about traditional farming practices, and enjoy the simplicity and beauty of rural living.

Whether seeking luxury, adventure, or a cultural connection, Scotland's unique accommodations offer something for every traveler. Each lodging type provides a distinct experience, allowing guests to engage with Scotland's history, nature, and culture in meaningful ways. These accommodations not only enhance the travel experience but also contribute to the preservation and celebration of Scotland's diverse heritage. By choosing unique accommodations, travelers can create lasting memories and gain a deeper appreciation for the rich tapestry of experiences that Scotland has to offer.

Local Workshops and Crafting

Scotland, with its rich heritage and vibrant culture, offers a plethora of opportunities for travelers to immerse themselves in the world of local craftsmanship and artisanal workshops. These experiences provide a unique insight into the traditional skills and creative processes that have been passed down through generations. Engaging with local artisans not only allows for a deeper understanding of Scottish culture but also offers the chance to create meaningful souvenirs that carry personal significance.

Nestled in the picturesque Highlands, the art of tartan weaving is a time-honored tradition that embodies Scotland's cultural identity. Visitors can participate in workshops at family-run mills, where they can learn about the intricate process of weaving this iconic fabric. Mill tours often include demonstrations of traditional loom techniques, providing a hands-on experience in crafting one's own piece of tartan. This immersive activity offers an appreciation for the skill and dedication required to produce the vibrant patterns that have come to symbolize Scottish heritage.

In the quaint village of Pitlochry, renowned for its bustling arts scene, pottery workshops invite travelers to explore the tactile world of clay. Under the guidance of skilled potters, participants can shape and glaze their own creations. These workshops often emphasize the connection between the land and the materials used, with local clay and natural pigments playing a prominent role. The satisfaction of molding a piece of art with one's own hands, coupled with the serene setting of the Scottish countryside, makes for a truly enriching experience.

The ancient craft of whisky barrel making, or cooperage, is another fascinating aspect of Scotland's artisanal landscape. In Speyside, home to some of the world's most famous whisky distilleries, visitors can engage in workshops that reveal the meticulous craftsmanship behind barrel construction. Cooperages offer demonstrations of traditional tools and techniques, allowing participants to try their hand at assembling a cask. This unique experience highlights the vital role that barrels play in the maturation process of whisky, adding depth to any whisky-tasting journey.

For those drawn to the art of jewelry making, Edinburgh's historic streets house numerous workshops where visitors can learn the delicate craft of silversmithing. Guided by experienced jewelers, participants can design and create their own bespoke pieces, often incorporating traditional Scottish motifs such as Celtic knots or thistles. These workshops not only offer a creative outlet but also serve as a gateway to understanding the cultural significance of jewelry as a means of storytelling and expression.

Exploring the Scottish Borders, one encounters a vibrant community of textile artists who specialize in the art of knitting and felting. Workshops in this region often focus on sustainable practices, using locally sourced wool and natural dyes. Participants can learn various techniques, from hand-knitting intricate patterns to felting vibrant landscapes. These sessions provide an opportunity to connect with the land and its resources, fostering an appreciation for the sustainable and ethical production of textiles.

In the coastal town of Oban, the ancient craft of boatbuilding is kept alive through interactive workshops. Visitors can join local craftsmen in constructing traditional wooden boats, learning about the techniques that have been used for centuries. These workshops often emphasize the importance of preserving maritime heritage, allowing participants to contribute to the restoration of historic vessels. The experience of working with wood and tools, combined with the salty sea air, creates a profound connection to Scotland's nautical past.

The art of Scottish cooking offers a deliciously immersive way to engage with local culture. Culinary workshops across the country invite participants to explore traditional recipes and cooking techniques. From baking bannocks on an open fire to crafting haggis from scratch, these sessions provide a hands-on introduction to Scotland's culinary heritage. Cooking with locally sourced ingredients, such as fresh seafood or Highland game, enhances the experience and offers a taste of Scotland's diverse flavors.

Engaging in local workshops and crafting experiences not only enriches one's understanding of Scottish culture but also supports the artisans and communities that keep these traditions alive. The personal connections formed during these encounters often lead to lasting memories and a deeper appreciation for the skills and stories that define Scotland's artistic landscape.

These workshops and crafting opportunities offer travelers a chance to step off the beaten path and discover the heart of Scotland's creative spirit. Whether weaving a piece of tartan, crafting a silver ring, or baking traditional bread, each experience is a testament to the enduring legacy of Scottish craftsmanship. By participating in these activities, travelers contribute to the preservation of cultural heritage, ensuring that these skills continue to thrive for future generations.

Through the lens of local craftsmanship, Scotland reveals itself as a tapestry of creativity, tradition, and innovation. Each workshop and crafting experience is a thread that weaves together the stories of the land and its people, inviting travelers to become part of this rich narrative. As you delve into the world of Scottish artisans, you'll find that the true essence of your journey lies not only in the creations you take home but in the connections and stories that stay with you long after you leave.

Seasonal Events and Celebrations

Scotland's seasonal events and celebrations offer a vibrant tapestry of cultural experiences, each one reflecting the nation's rich heritage and unique character. From traditional festivals that have been celebrated for centuries to contemporary gatherings that showcase Scotland's modern flair, these events provide a window into the country's soul. Participating in these celebrations allows visitors to engage with the local community, experience the diversity of Scottish culture, and create lasting memories.

The arrival of spring is marked by the colorful spectacle of Beltane Fire Festival, a modern reinterpretation of an ancient Celtic tradition celebrating the return of the sun. Held on Calton Hill in Edinburgh, this event draws a large crowd to witness a captivating performance of fire dancing, drumming, and storytelling. Participants paint their bodies in striking colors and don elaborate costumes, creating a visual feast that symbolizes the triumph of light over darkness. For those who enjoy immersive experiences, joining the festival as a performer or volunteer offers a deeper connection to its vibrant energy and communal spirit.

Summer in Scotland brings with it a wealth of outdoor events, with the Highland Games being a quintessential experience not to be missed. These traditional gatherings, held in towns and villages across the country, showcase Scotland's athletic prowess and cultural heritage. Events such as caber tossing, tug-of-war, and hammer throwing are accompanied by displays of Highland dancing and bagpipe music. The Braemar Gathering, attended by members of the royal family, is perhaps the most famous of these games, offering a unique blend of sportsmanship, pageantry, and camaraderie.

The long days of summer also set the stage for the Edinburgh Festival Fringe, the world's largest arts festival. This celebration of creativity transforms the city into a hub of artistic expression, with thousands of performances spanning theater, comedy, music, and dance. Street performers add to the lively atmosphere, entertaining passersby with their talents. For visitors, the Fringe offers an unparalleled opportunity to explore diverse artistic genres and discover emerging talents, making it a highlight of the summer season.

As autumn approaches, Scotland's landscapes burst into a kaleidoscope of colors, providing a stunning backdrop for seasonal celebrations. The Royal National Mòd, a festival dedicated to Gaelic language and culture, takes place in different locations each year, bringing together musicians, poets, and artists. Competitions in music, song, and literature highlight the richness of Gaelic tradition, while workshops and exhibitions offer insights into this vibrant cultural heritage. Attending the Mòd is a chance to experience the warmth and hospitality of Gaelic-speaking communities and to immerse oneself in Scotland's linguistic diversity.

Autumn is also the time for the Enchanted Forest, an award-winning sound and light show set in the woods of Faskally, near Pitlochry. This mesmerizing event transforms the forest into an otherworldly spectacle, with dazzling light installations and captivating music harmonizing with the natural surroundings. As visitors walk through the illuminated trails, they become part of a magical journey that celebrates the beauty of Scotland's landscapes. The Enchanted Forest offers a sensory experience that resonates with people of all ages, making it a favorite for families and nature lovers alike.

Winter in Scotland is marked by a series of festive celebrations that bring warmth and cheer to the darkest months. Hogmanay, Scotland's New Year celebration, is renowned for its lively street parties, fireworks, and traditional customs. Edinburgh's Hogmanay is the most famous, attracting visitors from around the world to enjoy live music, torchlight processions, and the spectacular midnight fireworks display over the castle. For a more intimate experience, smaller towns and villages host their own Hogmanay festivities, often featuring ceilidhs—traditional Scottish dances—where locals and visitors dance the night away.

The festive season continues with Burns Night, a celebration of Scotland's national poet, Robert Burns, held on January 25th. This event is marked by Burns suppers, where guests gather to enjoy haggis, recite Burns' poetry, and toast with whisky. The evening typically includes the "Address to a Haggis," a humorous ode to the dish, and ceilidh dancing. Burns Night offers a chance to experience Scottish hospitality and literary tradition in a convivial setting, making it a cherished annual celebration.

Throughout the year, Scotland's islands host a variety of unique festivals that reflect their distinct cultural identities. The Shetland Folk Festival, held in the spring, celebrates the islands' vibrant musical heritage with performances from local and international artists. The Orkney International Science Festival, taking place in early autumn, explores the intersection of science, heritage, and culture, featuring lectures, workshops, and exhibitions. These island festivals offer an opportunity to discover the diversity of Scotland's cultural landscape and to engage with the communities that call these remote regions home.

Scotland's seasonal events and celebrations offer a rich tapestry of experiences that invite travelers to connect with the country's cultural heritage and its people. Each event provides a unique lens through which to explore Scotland, from the ancient traditions of the Highland Games to the contemporary creativity of the Edinburgh Festival Fringe. By participating in these celebrations, visitors gain a deeper understanding of Scotland's identity and a chance to create cherished memories that last a lifetime. Whether experiencing the fiery exuberance of Beltane or the poetic warmth of Burns Night, Scotland's festivals are a testament to the enduring spirit and vibrant culture of this remarkable country.

CONCLUSION

Reflecting on Your Journey

Reflecting on a journey through Scotland is an invitation to revisit the myriad of experiences that have woven themselves into the fabric of your travels. Scotland, with its rugged landscapes, ancient castles, and vibrant culture, offers a kaleidoscope of memories that linger long after the journey has ended. Each corner of this enchanting land tells a story, and as you reflect, those stories become part of your own narrative.

From the moment you set foot in Scotland, the land itself becomes a character in your journey. The Highlands, with their sweeping vistas and mist-covered peaks, evoke a sense of awe and wonder. Driving through the winding roads, you may have felt the pull of the land, as if it were urging you to explore deeper, to uncover the secrets hidden in its glens and lochs. Perhaps you stood atop a windswept hill, the chill of the breeze on your face, and felt a connection to the countless travelers who have come before you, drawn by the same irresistible allure.

The cities of Scotland, each with its distinct personality, offer a vibrant counterpoint to the solitude of the countryside.

Edinburgh, with its historic architecture and lively arts scene, is a city that balances the past and present with grace. Wandering along the Royal Mile, you might have paused to listen to the strains of a street performer's bagpipe, the haunting melody weaving through the air. In Glasgow, the energy of the city pulses through its streets, where art and music thrive, and the warmth of its people invites you to join in the celebration of life.

The people you encountered on your journey likely left a lasting impression, their stories intertwining with your own. Whether it was the innkeeper who shared tales of local legends over a dram of whisky, or the artisan who invited you into their workshop to witness the creation of a handmade piece, these interactions enriched your experience. The Scots are known for their hospitality, and perhaps you found yourself embraced by their warmth, leaving you with a sense of belonging in this faraway land.

Reflections on your journey would be incomplete without revisiting the flavors and tastes that defined your culinary adventures. Scottish cuisine, with its emphasis on fresh, local ingredients, offers a feast for the senses. You may have savored the delicate taste of smoked salmon, the hearty comfort of a traditional Scotch broth, or the unique experience of tasting haggis for the first time. Each meal becomes a memory, a moment in time that captures the essence of Scotland's culinary heritage.

As you reflect, the traditions and celebrations you witnessed come to life once more. From the spirited energy of a Highland Games event, where athletes compete in feats of strength and agility, to the soulful melodies of a traditional ceilidh dance, these cultural experiences resonate with the rhythms of Scotland's heart. The echoes of bagpipes and the swirl of kilts in motion become vivid memories, a testament to the enduring spirit of the Scottish people.

Your journey through Scotland may have also been a personal exploration, a time to reconnect with yourself amidst the beauty and solitude of nature. The tranquility of a quiet walk along a deserted beach, the serenity of a misty morning in the glens, or the simple pleasure of a moment's reflection beside a still loch—each offered an opportunity to pause, to breathe, and to find clarity amidst the chaos of life.

Reflecting on your journey invites you to consider the lessons learned and the insights gained. Perhaps you discovered a newfound appreciation for history, a deeper connection to nature, or a rekindled sense of adventure. Scotland, with its rich tapestry of experiences, challenges you to see the world through new eyes, to embrace the unknown, and to find beauty in the unexpected.

As you look back on your time in Scotland, the memories you carry with you become a cherished part of your story. They are reminders of a land where the past and present coexist in harmony, where the landscapes are as diverse as the people who call it home. Scotland's magic lies in its ability to touch the soul, to inspire, and to leave an indelible mark on all who venture to its shores.

Your journey may have come to an end, but the reflections and memories continue to shape your path. The spirit of Scotland, with its wild beauty and rich traditions, remains with you, a constant companion on your life's journey. As you reflect, you carry the essence of Scotland with you—a reminder of a land that captured your heart and changed you in ways you never imagined.

BONUS 1: ESSENTIAL PHRASES FOR YOUR DAILY TRAVEL NEEDS IN SCOTLAND

BONUS 2: PRINTABLE TRAVEL JOURNAL

BONUS 3: 10 TIPS "THAT CAN SAVE THE DAY" ON YOUR TRIP IN SCOTLAND

Printed in Great Britain
by Amazon

59523607R00139